THE GEOGRAPHY BOOK

Activities for Exploring, Mapping, and Enjoying Your World

Caroline Arnold

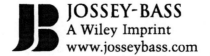
JOSSEY-BASS
A Wiley Imprint
www.josseybass.com

Published by Jossey-Bass
A Wiley Imprint
989 Market Street, San Francisco, CA 94103-1741   www.josseybass.com

Published simultaneously in Canada.

Illustrations copyright © 2002 by Tina Cash-Walsh.

Photographs on page 26 by Caroline Arnold.
Illustrations on pages 14, 22, 24, 32, 36, 38, 50, 53, 54, 55, 67, 79, 84, 90, and 98 based on drawings by Caroline Arnold.

Design and production by Navta Associates, Inc.

Jossey-Bass books and products are available through most bookstores. To contact Jossey-Bass directly call our Customer Care Department within the U.S. at 800-956-7739, outside the U.S. at 317-572-3986, or fax 317-572-4002.

Jossey-Bass also publishes its books in a variety of electronic formats. Some content that appears in print may not be available in electronic books.

Library of Congress Cataloging-in-Publication Data

Arnold, Caroline
   The geography book : activities for exploring, mapping, and enjoying your
world / Caroline Arnold
      p. cm.
   Includes bibiographical references (p.).
   ISBN 0-471-41236-8 (pbk. : alk. paper)
      1. Geography—Study and teaching (Elementary)—Activity programs. 1. Title.

G73 .A683 2001
910'.71'2—dc21   2001026802

Printed in the United States of America
FIRST EDITION
PB Printing   10 9

CONTENTS

INTRODUCTION

What Is Geography?

As you look out the window, you may see rolling hills, broad plains, mountains, a river valley, or perhaps the ocean. You also may notice what kinds of plants are growing, the weather, and what people are doing. The combination of landforms, vegetation, weather, and natural resources makes each place on Earth unique.

Geography is the study of the Earth and the processes that form it. It identifies places on the Earth, describes their physical features, and shows how they are connected to one another. It is also the study of people and how they influence and are influenced by their environment. Physical geography studies features of the Earth such as rivers, rocks, oceans, and the weather. Human geography studies how people use land for such things as settlement, farming, shipping, and transport. Tools that geographers use to gather information include maps, photographs, and computer databases.

Geography is one of the oldest sciences. Ancient Greeks who lived more than 2,000 years ago were among the earliest geographers. They gave us the word *geography,* which means "writing about the Earth." Descriptions of the Earth— both in words and in pictures—were particularly important in the past as early explorers, mapmakers, scientists, and others learned about new areas of the world. Their maps and writings about their travels helped establish trade routes and made it possible for people to travel and settle in many parts of the world.

The study of geography often overlaps with other scientific fields, including **geology, biology, anthropology,** and history. The special emphasis of geography that makes it different from other sciences is that it focuses on *where* things are. It also focuses on the human and environmental factors that help explain the ways that people, places, and things are distributed over the surface of the Earth.

Through the activities in this book, you will learn some basic facts about maps, one of the tools that geographers use to describe the Earth. You also will learn about the physical features of the Earth—its landmasses, bodies of water, and atmosphere.

Geography is part of our everyday lives. From road maps that help us get from one place to another to daily weather reports that help us decide whether to carry an umbrella, we depend on our knowledge of geography to get along in the world.

PART I

Find Yourself on Earth

In order to use maps and find your way around the Earth, you need to know how to find directions. In this part, you'll learn how to look at the stars to locate north and south and how to use a compass, and you'll discover how latitude and longitude can precisely pinpoint any place on Earth.

1

Which Way Is North?

If you imagine Earth rotating around a rod as it spins in space, the ends of that rod would stick out at what we call the North and South poles. The imaginary rod is Earth's **axis.** The poles are imaginary points used as references for measuring the location of places on Earth. The actual location of the North Pole is in the middle of the Arctic Ocean and is permanently covered with ice. The South Pole is just about in the center of the continent of Antarctica.

The North Star

The North Star, also called Polaris, is always directly over the North Pole. As Earth turns on its axis, other stars are seen in different places in the sky, but Polaris

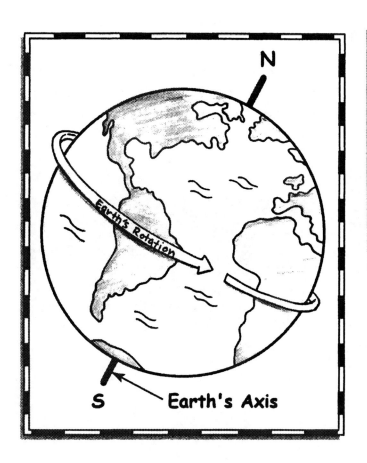

RACE TO THE POLES

In the late nineteenth and early twentieth centuries, there were many daring attempts to be the first person to reach the North and South poles. The remoteness, bitter cold, and fierce weather made traveling across the polar regions extremely dangerous. The first person credited with reaching the North Pole is American Robert E. Peary, who with his fellow explorer Matthew Henson and four Inuit raised the U.S. flag at the North Pole on April 6, 1909. The South Pole was reached two years later on December 14, 1911, by Norwegian Roald Amundsen, who had traveled across Antarctica by dogsled with four companions. About a month later a British expedition led by Robert F. Scott, traveling on foot by a different route, also reached the South Pole. Tragically, the Scott party perished on the return trip.

stays in the same spot. If you live in the northern hemisphere, you can figure out which direction is north by finding the North Star.

The North Star is in a constellation called Ursa Minor, which means "Little Bear" in Latin. Many people call this group of stars the Little Dipper because when the stars are connected like dots in a dot-to-dot picture, they look like a drinking cup with a long handle. It is close to another constellation called Ursa Major, the Big Bear, commonly known as the Big Dipper. As you may have figured out, the Big Dipper is shaped like the Little Dipper, only bigger. The Big Dipper is easy to spot because its stars are bright.

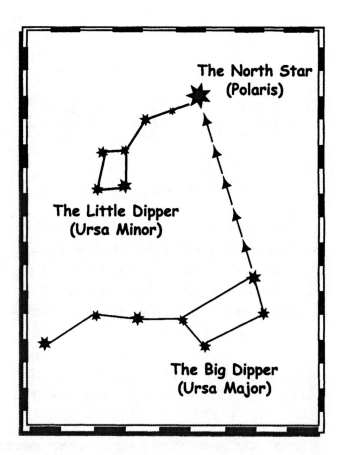

The North Star (Polaris)

The Little Dipper (Ursa Minor)

The Big Dipper (Ursa Major)

STAR DIRECTIONS

You will need:

a clear night and a place where you have a good view of the sky

1. Find the Big Dipper. Look for the two stars at the right side of the Big Dipper's cup. They are called the pointer stars.

2. Follow the path of these two stars up from the Big Dipper and you'll find the North Star, which is at the end of the handle of the Little Dipper.

Our names for the constellations come from the ancient Romans, who thought the groups of stars looked like the shapes of animals. Can you see the bear shapes of the Big Dipper and the Little Dipper? You will need to include some other nearby stars. What other shapes can you see in the sky?

The Big Dipper is also sometimes called the Drinking Gourd. Before and during the Civil War, it was an important guidepost for slaves from Southern states who were trying to escape to freedom in the North. When traveling at night, they looked for the Drinking Gourd and the North Star to know which way to go.

The Southern Cross

If you live in the southern hemisphere, you cannot see the North Star. Instead, you can find your direction by looking for a constellation called the Southern Cross, or Crux, its Latin name. It looks like a large cross in the sky. The Southern Cross is not at true south, but it is used as a reference that points to a much dimmer star, Sigma Octantis, that is almost exactly at true south. If you extend a line from the top to the bottom star of the Southern Cross and then continue the same distance four and half times, you will reach Sigma Octantis. The Southern Cross is visible on the horizon in the northern hemisphere as far north as Florida.

For thousands of years people all over the world have gazed at the stars and made up stories about them. Aboriginal people of Australia have several stories about the Southern Cross. Some believe that the pattern created by the stars is the footprint of a wedge-tailed eagle. Others believe that it is a stingray being pursued by a shark. Still others believe that the stars represent a clever man named Mirrabooka. What do they look like to you?

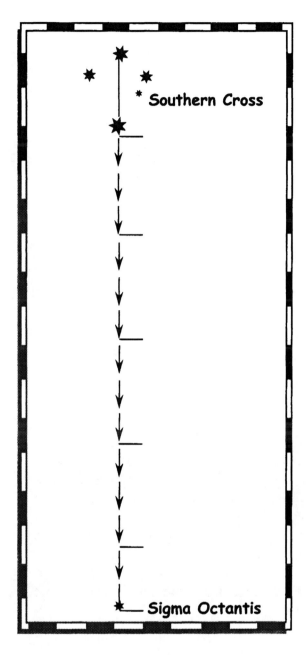

2

The Magnetic Poles

Earth's center is molten iron that acts like a giant magnet pulling at objects. Just like any magnet, it has north and south poles with lines of force connecting them. Earth's **magnetic poles** are close to, but not in exactly the same place as, the true or **geographic poles.**

The locations of Earth's magnetic poles have changed many times over the planet's long history. The north magnetic pole is currently in the area of the Queen Elizabeth Islands in northern Canada, about 1,000 miles from the north geographic pole. The south magnetic pole is currently in the vicinity of Wilkes Land, Antarctica, about 1,600 miles from the south geographic pole.

About 2,000 years ago the Chinese discovered that if they placed a small piece of magnetized iron ore on a reed or small piece of wood and floated it on water, the iron ore would always swing around and point north. They had created a simple **compass.** The iron ore that the Chinese used for their compass contained large amounts of a mineral called **magnetite.** Such rocks are also called **lodestones.** They are magnetized by natural processes during their formation.

A modern compass has a magnetized needle mounted inside a dial. You can use a compass to locate the direction of Earth's magnetic North and South poles. The iron needle in the center of the compass is mounted on a pivot so that it can swing freely. It will line up with the force of Earth's magnetism.

USING A COMPASS

You will need:

compass
marker
4 sheets of paper
transparent tape

1. Place the compass on a level spot in your bedroom and wait for the needle to stop moving. One end of the needle will point north. The other end will point south. (On most compasses, the pointed or longer end of the needle points north.)

2. Use the compass to find out the directions of your bedroom walls. Look at the needle of the compass to find north. Using the marker, write "N" for "north" on one sheet of paper and tape it to the wall that the needle is pointing to. When you face north, east will be on your right, west will be on your left, and south will be behind you.

3. Make direction labels for the other walls, and you will always know what direction you are facing.

3

Compass Rose

Most maps are drawn so that north is at the top. North is sometimes indicated by an arrow or an arrow with N at the top. You also may see a **compass rose** in the corner of a map. A compass rose points to all the directions. It is divided into 32 sections with emphasis on the eight major points—N, NE, E, SE, S, SW, W, NW. A compass rose gets its name because it looks like a flower with many pointed petals. You can make a giant compass rose on the sidewalk or your school playground.

MAKE A GIANT COMPASS ROSE

You will need:

chalk

a large paved area

compass

1. Using chalk, draw a large circle on the ground. (If your playground has a large circle already there, use it.)

2. Place the compass in the center of the circle, making sure that it is level. Wait until the needle is still, then turn the compass until the needle and the mark for north on the compass point the same way.

3. Draw a line from north on the compass to the edge of the circle and write "N" for "north." Using the compass as a guide, draw lines to the south, east, and west and write those directions at the edges of the circle.

4. Make additional marks for northeast, southeast, northwest, and southwest.

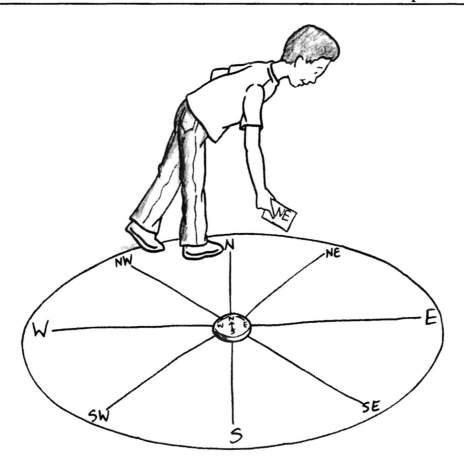

COMPASS ROSE RACE

You will need:

pencil
8 index cards
chalk
giant compass rose (see previous activity)
stopwatch, or watch with a second hand

1. Using the pencil, write each direction of your compass rose on a separate index card. You will have eight different cards marked N, NE, E, SE, S, SW, W, and NW. Mix up the cards and turn them face-down.

2. Use the chalk to draw a starting line about 30 feet from the compass rose (from the previous activity). One person (the timer) can use the watch to keep time while the other players each take a turn.

3. The timer says "Go" and starts counting to one minute. At the same time the first player draws a card. The player must run from the starting line to the compass rose and place the card on the spot noted on the card.

4. The same player then runs back to the starting line, picks another card, and places it on the compass rose. The player continues to pick up cards and place them on the compass rose until the timer says "Stop" or all the cards are placed.

5. All of the cards are collected, counted, and returned to the starting point. Then it's the next player's turn to see how many cards she can correctly place in a one-minute turn. Continue until all players have had a turn. The player with the most correctly placed cards in the shortest time wins the race.

4

Latitude and Longitude

In addition to showing the positions of the land and water, most maps and globes are also marked with lines of latitude and longitude. These lines form an imaginary grid that helps pinpoint the locations of places on Earth.

The lines of **latitude** (sometimes called parallels) circle the globe parallel to the **equator,** an imaginary line around the middle of the Earth that divides the northern and southern hemispheres. (*Hemi* means "half" in Greek, so a *hemisphere* is half a sphere or globe.) Latitude is measured in degrees according to the distance north or south of the equator, with the equator being 0 degrees and the poles 90 degrees.

The lines of **longitude** are the vertical

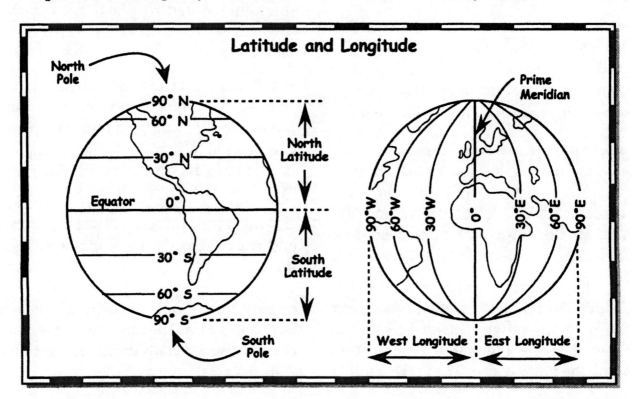

lines meeting at the North and South poles. There are 360 degrees of longitude around the Earth. They are measured east and west from the Prime Meridian in Greenwich, England, which is the zero point for calculating longitude. **Meridian** is another word for line of longitude. At the equator, each degree of longitude represents a distance of about 69 miles (115 km). As the lines of longitude approach the poles, the distance between them grows smaller until they meet. The **Prime Meridian** and the 180th longitude line are the dividing lines between the eastern and western hemispheres.

WHY GREENWICH?

Before the late 1800s, no standard systems were used for geographical measurements or for timekeeping. The facts that maps did not always use the same reference points and that clocks sometimes changed from town to town often confused travelers. So, in October 1884, 41 delegates from 25 nations met in Washington, D.C., for the International Meridian Conference. They decided to establish a single world meridian and that the zero point would be at the Royal Greenwich Observatory in England. Greenwich was chosen because maps based on calculations made at the Royal Observatory were already being used by nearly three-quarters of the world's seagoing vessels. Using the Greenwich meridian as a standard would cause the least disruption. The conference also voted to adopt a universal world day and a 24-hour clock, based on midnight at the Greenwich meridian.

Everywhere on Earth has its own particular latitude and longitude. They act as a global address. If you gave someone the precise latitude and longitude for your house, that person could find exactly where you live. Other places on Earth share the same latitude or the same longitude but not both. You can find out what other places share the same latitude and longitude with your city.

EXACTLY NORTH, SOUTH, EAST, AND WEST

You will need:

map or globe marked with lines of latitude and longitude
pencil
sheet of paper

1. Look at a map or globe and find the latitude and longitude of where you live.

2. Make a chart by drawing two lines across the sheet of paper to make a large cross. Mark the ends "N," "S," "E," and "W" to indicate directions. The horizontal line represents your latitude. Write the number of the latitude next to the line. The vertical line represents your longitude. Write the longitude number next to it.

3. Make a dot where the two lines meet and write the name of your city.

4. Use the map and follow your line of latitude east and west to find other places that lie on that latitude. Write their names on your chart in the order that they occur.

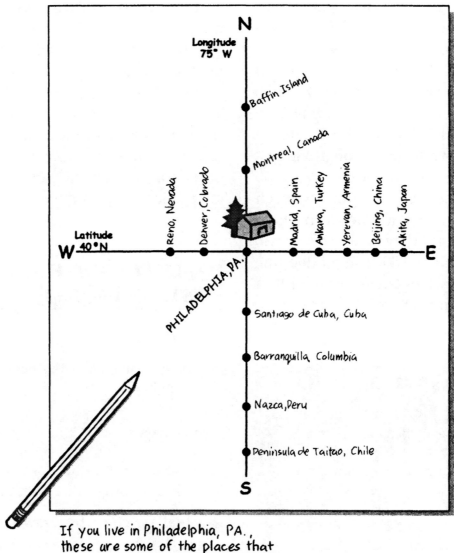

Longitude
75° W

N

Baffin Island

Montreal, Canada

Reno, Nevada

Denver, Colorado

Madrid, Spain

Ankara, Turkey

Yerevan, Armenia

Beijing, China

Akita, Japan

Latitude
40° N

W   E

PHILADELPHIA, PA.

Santiago de Cuba, Cuba

Barranquilla, Columbia

Nazca, Peru

Peninsula de Taitao, Chile

S

If you live in Philadelphia, PA.,
these are some of the places that
have the same latitude or longitude.

Then follow your line of longitude north and south, and write down names of places that you find. Now you know a few places that are exactly north, south, east, and west from where you live.

At the Royal Observatory in Greenwich, England, there is mark showing 0 degrees longitude. If you straddle the line, you can be in both the eastern and western hemispheres at the same time! In Ecuador in South America there is a large marker for the equator. If you stand on either side of it, you can be in both the northern and southern hemispheres at the same time! Can you guess how the country of Ecuador got its name? What other countries of the world are on the equator?

PART II

Mapping the Earth

Maps are guides to the world we live in. They show where people live, what they do, how to travel, what is happening with the weather, the shape of the land, and many other things. Maps vary from simple sets of directions to detailed descriptions of a particular place at a particular time. Maps help us understand how and why the world is different from place to place and over time.

People have been making and using maps for a long time. The oldest known map was made over 4,000 years ago in ancient Babylon. Even before that, prehistoric people may have made maps to show where to find food and water. Later, explorers needed maps so they wouldn't get lost as they traveled to distant places. Traders needed maps to know where to sell their goods. Kings and soldiers needed maps to rule their kingdoms and to plan battles. The first maps were not very good, but as people found out more about the world, their maps became better.

There are many different kinds of maps. Some show political boundaries, such as countries, states, and cities, while others show the physical features of the land. Maps show the location of natural resources, industries, weather patterns, distributions of people and wildlife, and a wide range of other information about Earth and its inhabitants. Maps are a kind of diagram, or shorthand, that describes the physical world and its relationship to people and events.

Most maps tell us about the modern world, but maps are also important for showing the way things were in the past. For instance, maps can help us understand the extent of ancient civilizations, trace the sea routes of early explorers, and see what the world was like when dinosaurs were alive. Maps, such as those used to forecast weather or to predict population growth, also can help us plan for the future.

People who make maps are called **cartographers.** Their goal is to present information so that it is clear, accurate, and, in many cases, beautiful too. **Cartography** includes all stages of mapmaking, from gathering information to printing or drawing the map. Modern technology—such as aerial photography, satellite imaging, and radar—is helping to make maps more accurate. Modern mapmakers also use computers to do many of the calculations that used to be done by hand.

5

The Earth Is Round

Ancient Greek geographers knew that the Earth was round, but it wasn't until the 1400s that explorers actually sailed around the Earth and showed that this was true. It is hard to see that the Earth is round because obstacles on land make it difficult to detect the shape of the horizon. But on a clear day at sea, you can look over the water and see the curve of the Earth.

Another way to see the shape of the Earth is to look at a globe. A **globe** is a tiny model of Earth as it would look if you were able to view it from space. The equator circles the globe halfway between the North and South poles. The greatest distance around Earth is at the equator. If you traveled around the Earth at the equator, you would go about 25,000 miles (40,076 km).

A BALLOON GLOBE

You will need:

round balloon (blue is best)
permanent marker
map or globe
piece of heavy paper (such as a file folder)
scissors

1. Blow up the balloon and tie a knot in it. The knot will be the South Pole of your globe.

2. Using the marker, draw an X at the top of the balloon opposite the knot. This will be the North Pole.

3. Now draw a line around the center of the balloon halfway between the poles. This is the equator.

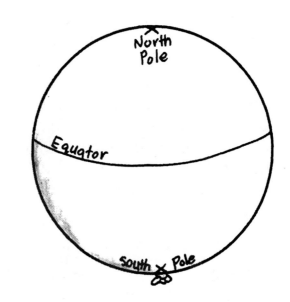

17

4. Draw the continents on your balloon globe, using a map or globe as a guide. You may want to add more details, such as major cities and landmarks.

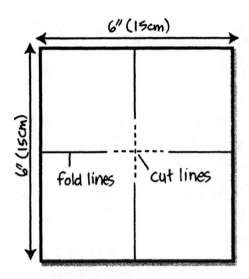

6" (15cm)

6" (15cm)

fold lines cut lines

5. To make a stand for your balloon globe, cut a 6-by-6-inch (15-by-15-cm) square out of the heavy paper. Fold the square in half and make a small cut about ½ inch long in the center. Unfold the paper and fold it in half in the other direction. Make another small cut across the center. When you open the paper you will have a small cut in the shape of an X. Slip the knot of the balloon through the X. Now your balloon globe will stand by itself.

The first known globe was made in ancient Greece more than 2,000 years ago. It was 6½ feet (2.3 m) in diameter! The oldest existing globe was made by Martin Behairn in Nuremberg, Germany, in 1492. It is 21 inches (52.5 cm) in diameter. Like other early globes, it contained many mistakes because much of the world was unexplored at that time.

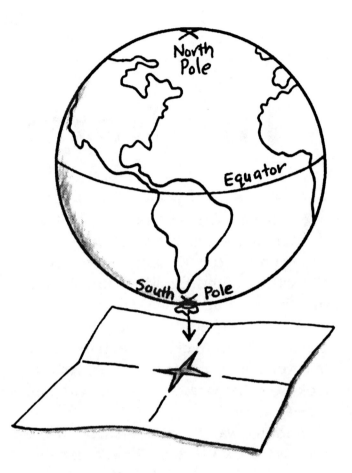

North Pole

Equator

South Pole

HOW FAR AROUND THE EARTH?

The first scientific measurement of the distance around the Earth was probably made about 2,000 years ago by a Greek astronomer named Eratosthenes. Using the difference of the angle of the Sun at noon on the first day of summer between Alexandria, where he lived, and the city of Syene (now Aswan) directly to the south, he calculated the distance around the Earth to be about 27,750 miles (46,250 km). Even though Eratosthenes' instruments were not as accurate as those used today, his measurement was remarkably close to the actual distance around the Earth.

Making the Round Earth Flat

One of the problems for mapmakers is how to make an accurate flat map of a round object such as the Earth. One solution is to draw the map in narrow sections called **gores.** Each gore is like a section of the Earth between two lines of longitude. The top and the bottom of the gore come to a point at the poles. The center is widest at the equator. This type of map comes close to showing everything at the same relative size but sometimes can be hard to read because of the spaces between the gores.

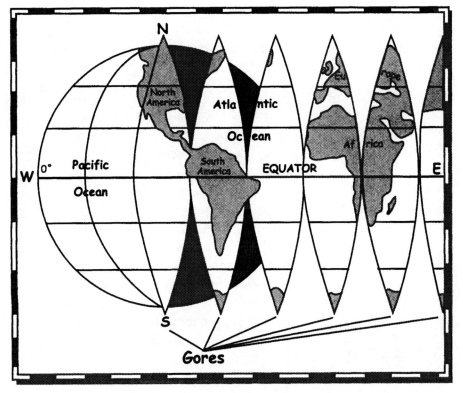

Gores

ORANGE PEEL EXPERIMENT

Cut and peel an orange and make your own gores to see how this method is used to make world maps.

You will need:

globe

permanent marker

one orange (choose a type that peels easily)

table knife

19

1. Using a globe as a guide, draw the equator and the outlines of the continents on the skin of the orange. The North Pole should be where the stem of the orange was attached.

2. Use the knife to cut just through the skin of the orange, making two circles that intersect at the poles and divide the orange into quarters.

3. Now carefully peel the skin off the orange. Put the pieces side by side. Do they look something like the map on page 19?

Another way to make a flat map of the Earth is to "stretch" parts of it.

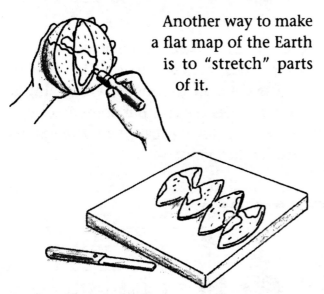

STRETCHING THE GLOBE

You can see how maps of the world become distorted when they are flattened by cutting apart a balloon globe and stretching it.

You will need:

balloon globe (see chapter 5)
scissors

1. Let the air out of the balloon globe by cutting off the knot.

2. Carefully cut the balloon from the South Pole (at the knot) to the North Pole (at the top of the balloon). A good place to make the cut is through the Pacific Ocean.

3. Stretch each side of the balloon and try to make it flat. You can see that the shapes of the continents change a lot at the edges of the balloon and that distances between places seem to grow larger.

4. Try cutting out Australia and stretching it to make it flat. This is much easier to do than stretching the whole globe because each small area is relatively flat.

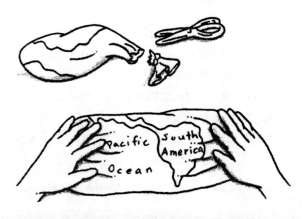

Mapmakers transfer information about the curved surface of the Earth onto a flat surface by making a **projection**. Using complicated mathematical calculations, mapmakers figure out relative distances from a chosen starting point. It is impossible to make every part on a map to an equal scale, so map projections always have some distortion—as if parts of the globe were being stretched. Some projections distort shapes and directions badly but show the relative sizes of areas correctly. Others distort sizes but show shapes and directions correctly. Mapmakers have developed more than 100 different projections. The projection chosen for a particular map depends on the purposes of the map.

7

Time Zones of the World

It takes 24 hours, or one day, for Earth to make one complete turn, or revolution, in space. As each hour passes, Earth rotates approximately 15 degrees of longitude. At the 1884 International Meridian Conference, it was agreed to divide the world into 24 time zones of 15 degrees each, measured from the Prime Meridian in Greenwich, England. All other times around the world are based on the time set in Greenwich, called Greenwich Mean Time. The halfway point around the Earth, centered on the 180th meridian, is called the **International Date Line.** This is the point at which one day ends and a new day begins. The lines separating the time zones do not always follow the meridians exactly. Some of the divisions have been shifted to keep countries or communities in the same zone. In some parts of the world, such as India and central Australia, the zones vary on the half hour so that noon occurs when the Sun is at the highest point in the sky.

WHY DAYLIGHT SAVING?

Daylight Saving Time, which moves clock time one hour ahead of Sun time, was used for the first time during World War I as a means of saving energy. (People slept in the morning when it was dark and had one more hour of sunlight in the evening before they needed to turn on lights and turn up their furnaces.) Daylight Saving Time was so unpopular that it was stopped after seven months. Daylight Saving Time was used again during World War II and after that in some states during the summer months. In 1966 the U.S. Congress passed a law establishing a uniform system of daylight saving for the whole country. Today many countries have Daylight Saving Time in the summer so that people have more time after school and work to enjoy the summer sunshine.

MAKE A WORLD CLOCK

You can make a "clock" that will help you figure out what time it is in other parts of the world.

21

You will need:

scissors   pen

2 paper plates   brad

ruler

1. Cut the rim off one paper plate to make a flat circle.

2. Use the ruler and pen to divide the circle into 24 equal pie-shape sections. Start by dividing the circle into quarters and divide these in half to make eighths. Then divide each of these into three smaller sections.

3. Write "London, Greenwich Mean Time" in one of the sections. Then, con-

Cities of the World by Time Zone

London
(Greenwich Mean Time)

Paris

Cairo

Moscow

Tiblisi

Yekaterinburg

Tashkent

Jakarta

Beijing

Tokyo

Sydney

Magadan

Wellington

Samoa

Honolulu

Anchorage

Los Angeles

Denver

Chicago

Washington

Santiago

Rio de Janiero

Atlantic Ocean

Greenland

tinuing clockwise, use the list below and write the name of each city in one of the sections.

4. Place the circle with the city names on top of the other paper plate. Fasten them together in the center with the brad.

5. On the rim of the plate, above the pie section that says "London," write "12:00 MIDNIGHT." Continue in a clockwise manner, writing 1:00 A.M., 2:00 A.M., 3:00 A.M., and so on, above each pie section. When you reach 12:00, write "12:00 NOON." Continue with 1:00 P.M., 2:00 P.M., 3:00 P.M., and so on, until you come back to "12:00 MIDNIGHT."

6. Look at the time on the rim above the time zone where you live. That is what time it is when it is 12:00 midnight in London. When you rotate the circle so that the time on the rim is your current time, the other pie sections will tell you what time it is in other cities in the world.

8

Maps to Scale

A map is a model of a place. It shows what the place is like, but it's much smaller than the real thing. A map as large as a page of this book can represent a room, a region, the world, or even the whole universe.

The **scale** of a map tells you how much smaller the map is than what it shows. One inch or 1 centimeter may represent a short distance or a very long distance. On a large-scale map, 1 inch or 1 centimeter represents just a few miles or kilometers. The larger the scale of the map, the more details you can see. When 1 inch represents more than 16 miles or 1 centimeter represents more than 20 kilometers, the map is usually considered to have a small scale. It is like a distant view of the Earth's surface.

Sometimes maps of big areas have smaller maps within them that are drawn to a larger scale. The small map is called an **inset.** It usually shows a small but important part of the area in greater detail.

Architects and designers use floor plans to show how the rooms in buildings are arranged and how the furniture can be positioned. In many ways these plans are like large-scale maps. You can make a scale-model drawing, or plan, of a room in your house. To do so, you will have to convert the actual measurements of the room to the scale of your model.

MAKE A ROOM PLAN

You will need:

measuring tape
paper and pencil for notes
large sheet of heavy paper or poster board
ruler or yardstick
medium-size sheet of paper
scissors

1. Measure the length and width of the room. Write down the measurements on the note paper.

2. For your model, you will be using 1 foot to equal 1 inch. Change the units of the measurements you made from feet to inches. To change measurements that are already in inches, add ¼ inch for every 3 inches. For example, 7 feet 6 inches would equal 7½ inches. (If you are using metric measurements, your scale will be 1 meter to 10 centimeters. To convert your measurements, simply move the decimal place to the left. For example, a room that is 6.3 meters wide would be 63 centimeters wide in your drawing.)

3. Draw the outline of the room on the large sheet of paper using the ruler or yardstick to mark the distances to scale. Measure the locations of doors and windows in the room and draw those to scale on the plan. When you are finished, your drawing will be like a bird's-eye view of the room.

4. Measure other objects in the room—such as rugs, chairs, and bookcases—and draw those to scale on a separate sheet of paper. Cut them out and place them on your plan. Try different arrangements to see which one you like the best.

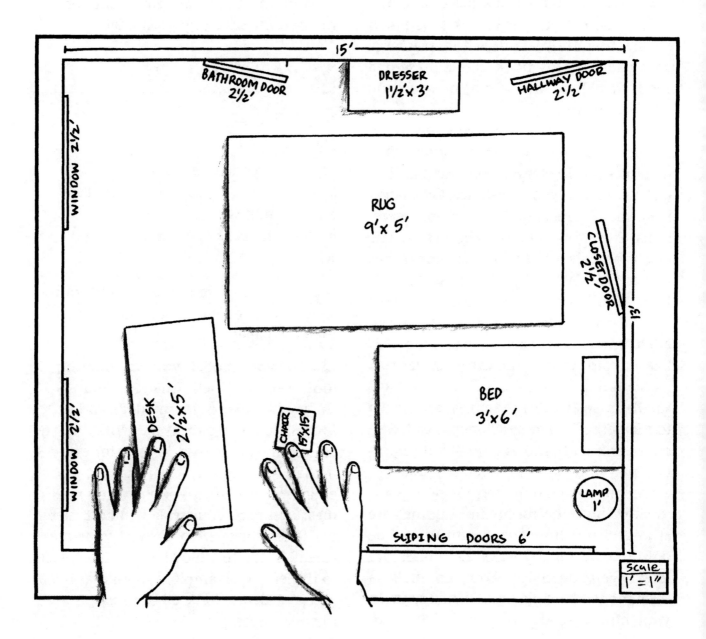

9

Photo Maps

In many ways a map is like a picture of a place taken from the sky. Mapmakers often use **aerial photos**—photos taken from the air—to make maps more accurate. Sometimes maps are actually created from photos taken from airplanes or from satellites in space.

You can get an idea about how photos are useful to mapmakers by making a photo collage. A collage is created from several elements. You also will discover why it is difficult to use photos to make a map.

MAKE A PANORAMIC PHOTO

You will need:

camera and film
large sheet of paper
transparent tape
permanent marker

1. Go to the top of a tall building that has windows or a viewing platform where you can look at the ground below. Use the camera to take pictures of the ground. Move around the building as far as you can taking photos as you go. Try to over- lap the edges of the areas you are photo- graphing. (Doing so will help you match the photos after you get them developed.) If you have film left over, you might want to take pictures of some local landmarks.

2. Take the film to a developer and have prints made. Spread out the prints on the large sheet of paper. Arrange them side by side in the order that you took them, over- lapping the edges where they match. Notice that the edges of objects don't always match up perfectly. That's because the angle of your view when you were tak- ing the photos changed as you moved. If you were able to go around the whole building, you will end up with a circle that looks something like a large doughnut. The "hole" in the doughnut is the build- ing where you took the photos. If you could see only partway around the build- ing from your viewing spot, you will have a line or semicircle of photos.

3. Tape the photos together to make one continuous photo. Tape the large photo to the paper. Use the marker to write names of streets and other landmarks. Use your knowledge of the area to note special places and directions. Is your panoramic photo something like a map?

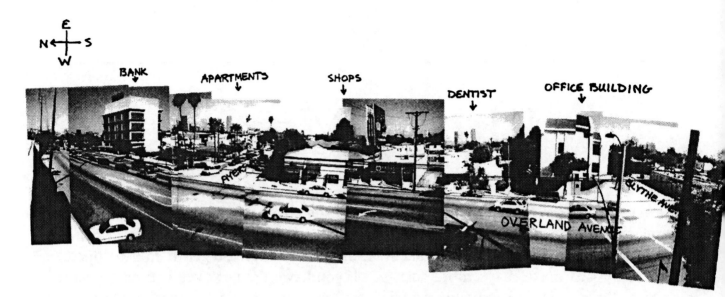

RANCHO PARK
(view from top of parking garage)

MAPS VERSUS PHOTOS

There are many reasons why having a map can be better than having a photograph of a location. On a map, you can mark the names and numbers of roads and highways. A map also can make some things more visible than others. For example, a map can show only where mountains and deserts are located and not include any roads. It also can eliminate unnecessary objects, such as trees and fences, that get in the way of seeing the ground. A photograph includes only features that can be seen. However, a map can show underground features, such as subways or layers of rock. It also can show invisible boundaries, such as state borders or city limits.

10

Map Keys Unlock Map Secrets

Most maps are written in a kind of code. Colors, letters, numbers, and other symbols represent important places in the community and features of the landscape. Each kind of map has its own symbols. Topographic maps have symbols showing elevation. Weather maps have symbols showing temperature, precipitation, and barometric pressure. Road maps have symbols for different types of roads and various tourist attractions.

Small circles or dots are often used to represent cities and towns. Sometimes the size of the dot reflects the population of the city, with bigger cities having larger dots. Sometimes a star within a circle is used to represent the capital of a state or country.

MAP KEY
🏠 My house
🏫 School
📖 Library
🛒 Store
Pool
= = Road
Trail
Tree

27

Lines on maps usually are used to represent roads, boundaries, rivers, and railroads. Hatch marks across a line usually indicates a railway. Dotted lines often represent boundaries. Different colors and widths of lines can indicate different kinds of roads.

Pictures, such as an airplane for an airport, a tree for a park, a table for a picnic area, or a flag for a post office, also are used as map symbols.

The **map key** explains what the symbols on a particular map mean. It is usually placed in a box in a corner of the map. Map keys are also sometimes called **legends.**

Here is a map of a community. What symbol has been used to represent schools? How many schools do you see?

THE KEY TO YOUR NEIGHBORHOOD

You will need:

sheet of paper
pen or pencil

1. Draw a map of your neighborhood.

2. Create your own map symbols to represent your school, where your friends live, different kinds of shops and businesses, movie theaters, parks and playgrounds, and whatever else you want to show.

3. Make a map key in the corner of your map to show what the symbols represent.

11

Relief Maps

The height, or **elevation,** of landmasses on the Earth is measured according to their distance above sea level. Because the ocean is continuous, its surface is at about the same height throughout the world. Essentially, sea level is the shoreline of the ocean. However, because the ocean's surface is constantly disturbed by winds, currents, tides, changes in temperature, and other factors it is never exactly flat. To get a standard measurement for sea level, scientists measure the ocean at various locations over a period of time and then average the measurements.

Most people live in places that are within a few hundred feet (100 m) of sea level. Do you know what the elevation of your community is?

Most maps of the Earth are drawn on flat paper. But this does not give a realistic picture because the surface of the Earth isn't flat. Three dimensional (3-D) maps, or **relief maps,** are one way to show the height of the land. The scale on most relief maps is exaggerated—mountains are taller, valleys are deeper—to emphasize the differences in elevation.

You can make a 3-D map that shows where there are mountains and valleys.

MAKE A 3-D MAP

You will need:

cardboard about 12 inches (30 cm) square

aluminum foil

2 cups sawdust

⅓ cup wallpaper paste (available at a hardware store)

about 8 ounces (.25 liter) of water

large bowl

tempera paint (various colors)

paintbrushes

1. Cover the cardboard with aluminum foil.

LIVING AT SEA LEVEL

In the Netherlands, which means "low lands," much of the land is at or below sea level. People have built large dikes along the coast as barriers to keep sea water from flooding the land. Beginning in the 1600s the Dutch people used windmills to pump water out of lakes and marshes behind the dikes and drained the land so that they could grow crops.

29

2. Put the sawdust, wallpaper paste, and water in the bowl. Mix it with your hands to make a stiff clay.

3. Use the clay to make your map on the foil. Your map can be of a real or an imaginary place. If it is a real place, use a map that shows the elevations of the land as a guide.

4. When your clay map is done, let it dry. This will take a few days. Then you can paint it.

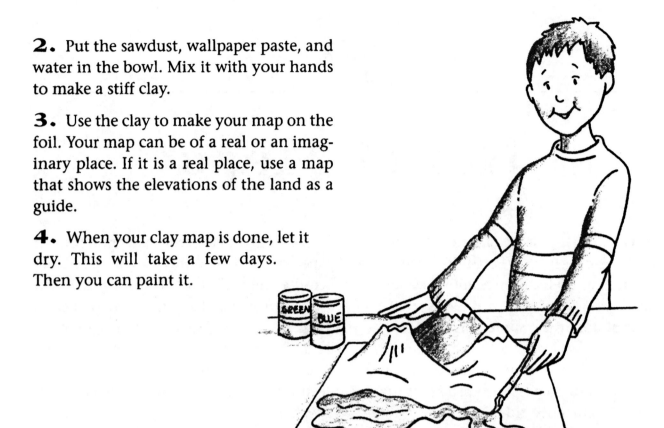

HOW BUMPY IS THE EARTH?

The top of Earth's highest mountain, Mount Everest in Tibet, reaches more than 5 miles (8 km) above sea level. The greatest ocean depth, at the bottom of the Mariana Trench in the Pacific Ocean, is about 6.8 miles (11 km) below sea level. Yet compared to the whole surface of the Earth, these are relatively small variations in its overall elevation.

Imagine that Earth is as small as an orange. When you hold an orange in your hand, the skin feels smooth. But if you look at the skin through a magnifying glass, you can see that there are many little bumps and hollows. They are somewhat like the valleys and mountains on Earth. Earth's land also looks smooth from a distance. It is only when you are close that you can see its varied surface.

Color-Coded and Contour Maps

Color-coded maps are a way to show changes in elevation without 3-D. Usually blue is used for water, green is used for lowlands, yellow is used for low hills, brown is used for high hills, and red or white is used for the tallest mountains. The map key tells exactly what each color represents. By looking at the gradation of colors across the map, you can get an idea of the shape of the land.

Another way to show how the land is shaped is with a **contour map.** A contour map depicts the surface of the Earth with a series of lines connecting places of equal elevation. Every point along each line has the identical height above sea level. Closely spaced contour lines indicate a steep slope. Lines spaced far apart show relatively flat land. On contour maps of large areas, the lines meet to form loops. A series of nestled loops—looking something like the rings of a target—indicates a hill.

You can draw contour lines around a potato to see how the landforms on an island might be mapped.

CONTOUR POTATO

You will need:

table knife
large potato
plate
thin-tipped permanent marking pen
ruler

1. Cut the potato in half lengthwise. Place the cut side down on the plate.

2. Sit or kneel so that you are eye level with the potato. Use the pen to draw lines around the potato, rotating the plate as you draw. Each line should follow the same elevation, beginning about ¼ inch from the surface of the plate. Use the ruler to check your measurements. Make each line about ¼ inch higher than the one before it. If you are using metric measurements, make the lines about 1 centimeter apart.

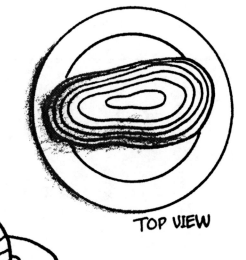

TOP VIEW

3. Look down at the potato from directly above. Do you see a series of rings around the potato? Do they look like the lines on a contour map of an island? What is the steepest part of your potato?

SIDE VIEW

THE OCEAN FLOOR

The first contour maps were made in the eighteenth century. They were of places *below* sea level. Sailors needed to know the shape of the land under the sea so their ships did not run aground.

The bottom of the ocean is just as varied as the surface of the land. It has mountains, plains, canyons, plateaus, basins, and other features similar to those found on land. The deepest parts of the ocean are narrow chasms called trenches. The greatest known depth is the Challenger Deep of the Mariana Trench in the Pacific Ocean.

UNITED STATES GEOLOGICAL SURVEY

The United States Geological Survey (USGS) is an agency of the U.S. government that was founded in 1879 to evaluate the nation's mineral and water resources, to survey and map the country's physical features, and to supervise the leasing of federal lands for mining and gas and oil exploration. Since that time, the USGS has made topographic, or contour, maps of almost every part of the United States. These maps, which have been prepared to exacting standards of accuracy, are available in a variety of scales. USGS topographic maps are used by hikers and campers as well as by community planners, engineers, and other businesspeople. You may be able find topographic maps of your area at a store that sells camping supplies, or go to the web site topozone.com to get an interactive topographic map of the United States. Other topographic map sites can be located from the USGS home page (www.usgs.gov).

13

Road Maps

When American pioneers went west to Oregon, they knew which way to go. They followed the Oregon Trail, which was just a dirt track through the wilderness, and the trip took months by horse and wagon. Today people travel on a huge network of freeways and highways and can go hundreds of miles in just a few hours. Roads make it easier for people to travel from one place to another, but travel wouldn't be so easy if we didn't have maps showing where all those roads go.

PLANNING A TRIP

You will need:

road map or road atlas
clear plastic sheet (such as a notebook sheet protector)
thin-tipped permanent marking pen

1. Using a map or a road atlas, choose a starting point and destination for a trip that you would like to take.

2. Cover the map with the plastic sheet.

3. Using the marker, trace your route.

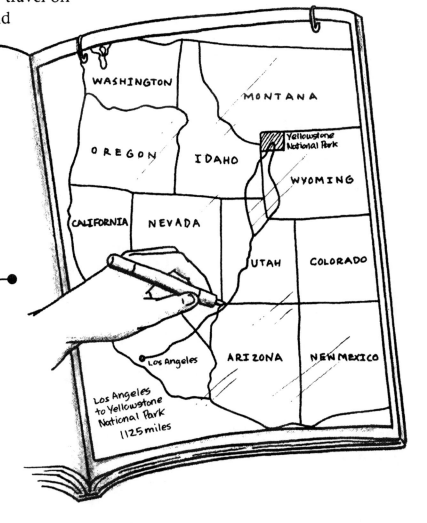

33

4. Figure out the approximate distance between the beginning and end of your journey by adding up the mileage numbers along your route or by using the mileage guide in the map key.

5. Assuming an average speed of 50 miles per hour, how long would it take you to reach your destination? (*Hint:* Divide the total number of miles by 50.)

INTERSTATE HIGHWAYS

The roads of the interstate highway system in the United States form a grid across the nation with nine main east/west routes and ten north/south routes. The east/west routes have even numbers and begin with I-10 going across the southern states, joining Los Angeles and Miami, and end with I-90 across the northern states. The north/south routes have odd numbers and begin with I-5 going along the West Coast of the country and end with I-95 going along the East Coast. The construction of the interstate system was authorized by the Federal Aid Highway Act of 1956 under President Dwight D. Eisenhower. Its purpose was to make travel between the states faster, safer, and more direct.

14

Weather Maps

Weather maps provide information about the weather over large regions of the country or world. They show the location of high- and low-pressure systems and the leading edge, or front, of a mass of warm or cold air. Areas of high pressure, which usually mean fair weather, are marked with an "H," and areas of low pressure, which usually bring rain, are marked with an "L." A warm front usually is represented by a line with semicircles pointing in the direction in which the front is moving. A cold front is represented by a line with triangles. **Isotherms** are the lines connecting areas of the same temperature. **Isobars** are lines connecting regions of the same atmospheric pressure. Isotherms and isobars resemble the lines of a contour map. Weather maps also include information about cloudiness, precipitation, and wind speed and direction. You can look in your newspaper for a weather map for your region.

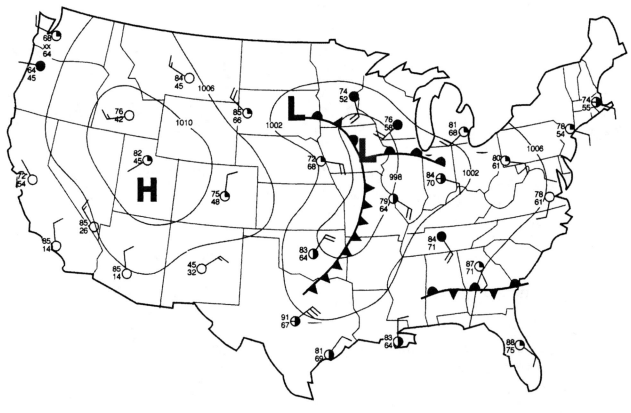

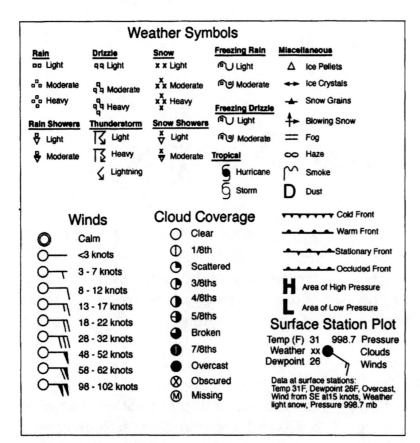

Weather Symbols

Rain		Drizzle		Snow		Freezing Rain		Miscellaneous	
ᵖᵖ	Light	ᵠᵠ	Light	x x	Light	⌒∪	Light	△	Ice Pellets
ᵖᵖ	Moderate	ᵠᵖ	Moderate	x x	Moderate	⌒∪	Moderate	↔	Ice Crystals
ᵖᵖ	Heavy	ᵠᵖ	Heavy	x x	Heavy			↟	Snow Grains

Rain Showers		Thunderstorm		Snow Showers		Freezing Drizzle			
▽	Light	⊾	Light	▽	Light	⌒∪	Light	✚	Blowing Snow
▽	Moderate	⊾	Heavy	▽	Moderate	⌒∪	Moderate	═	Fog
		∠	Lightning			Tropical		∞	Haze
						ϟ	Hurricane	⌒	Smoke
						ϟ	Storm	D	Dust

Winds

○	Calm
○—	<3 knots
○—┬	3 - 7 knots
○—┬	8 - 12 knots
○—┬┬	13 - 17 knots
○—┬┬	18 - 22 knots
○—┬┬┬	28 - 32 knots
○—┬┬┬┬	48 - 52 knots
○—┬┬┬┬┬	58 - 62 knots
○—◤	98 - 102 knots

Cloud Coverage

○	Clear
◐	1/8th
◖	Scattered
◑	3/8ths
◐	4/8ths
◓	5/8ths
●	Broken
◕	7/8ths
●	Overcast
⊗	Obscured
Ⓜ	Missing

〰〰〰 Cold Front

▲▲▲▲ Warm Front

〰▲〰▲ Stationary Front

▲●▲● Occluded Front

H Area of High Pressure

L Area of Low Pressure

Surface Station Plot

Temp (F) 31   998.7 Pressure
Weather xx ●   Clouds
Dewpoint 26   Winds

Data at surface stations:
Temp 31F, Dewpoint 26F, Overcast,
Wind from SE at 15 knots, Weather
light snow, Pressure 998.7 mb

2. Draw one of the following symbols on the inside of each circle: sun, cloud, sun covered by half of a cloud, lightning, rain, tree bending in the wind, snow.

3. Color each symbol with the markers and cut it out.

4. Glue a magnet to the back of each weather symbol.

5. Look at the weather forecast in the newspaper or listen to the weather report on radio or television. Place the appropriate weather magnets for the next day's weather on your refrigerator. Everyone in your family will know what kind of weather to expect the next day.

WEATHER MAGNETS

You can make up your own weather symbols and give your family a daily weather report with a set of weather symbol magnets.

You will need:

pencil

bottle cap or 50-cent coin

heavy paper (such as a file folder)

colored markers

scissors

white glue

small magnets (you can get these at a craft store)

1. Trace around the bottle cap or 50-cent coin to make seven circles out of heavy paper.

15

Dot Maps

Any kind of numerical information that varies from place to place—such as the size of the population or amount of natural resources—can be shown on a map. One way to show the differences in quantity is with dots, letting each dot represent a certain amount of real units. For instance, you can make a map of how many bushels of corn were produced in each county in Iowa by using one dot to represent 1,000 bushels of corn. Counties producing the most corn will have the most dots on your map. Dot maps are a good way to show this kind of information at a glance.

You can make a dot map showing the distribution of people in your state.

STATE POPULATION MAP

You will need:

tracing paper, about 9 by 12 inches (24 by 30 cm)

map of your state, about 9 by 12 inches (24 by 30 cm)

4 paper clips

marking pen

paper punch

index card

list of the towns and cities in your state and their populations (look in an atlas or on a state road map)

pencil

sheet of paper

1. Lay the tracing paper on top of the map and fasten it in place with the paper clips.

2. Use the marking pen to trace the outline of the state.

3. Punch a hole in a corner of the index card. This hole will be the stencil for making dots on your map.

4. Look at the list of towns and cities in your state. Using the pencil and paper, make a list of those with populations of more than 10,000.

5. Locate each town on the map, and make a dot on the tracing paper over the town by drawing over the stencil hole with the marking pen. Each dot represents 10,000 people. For towns larger than 10,000, add as many dots as necessary to show the total population, rounding off to the nearest 10,000. For instance, a town of 32,000 would have three dots and a town of 97,000 would have ten dots. Overlap the dots of larger towns to make a cluster.

When you are finished, your map will show the population clusters in your state. What is the closest population center to where you live?

16

Old and New Maps

Maps change as communities change. People move, roads and bridges are built, and buildings are erected and torn down. As the world changes, maps need to be updated so that they are accurate. Look in your library for atlases or other books with maps in them that were published more than ten years ago. Can you find countries that have different names or different borders than they do now? The continent of Africa has had many changes in the last half century. Can you find out what used to be the names for Zaire, Zambia, and Zimbabwe?

Maps provide a record of human activity and help us to understand events in relation to the places where they occurred. They may show the locations of battles,

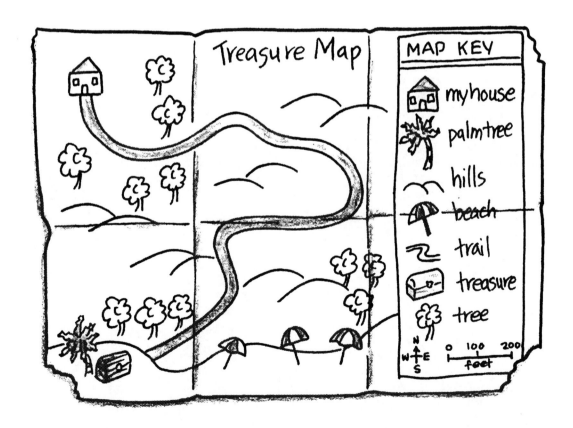

national borders at a particular moment in time, or the routes of ancient explorers. They may even show the location of buried treasure.

You can make a map that looks like an old pirate map. It can be a pretend map, or you may really want to hide some "treasure" and then make a map that gives directions how to find it.

BURIED TREASURE

You will need:

sheet of white paper
½ cup cold coffee
brown or black permanent marker

1. First tear a small strip off each edge of the paper to give your map ragged edges. Then crumple the paper into a ball. Now smooth it out to make it flat again.

2. Dip the edges of the paper in the coffee. They will turn brown. Let them dry.

3. Now use the marker to draw a map in the middle of the paper. Add a map key to show which way is north, a scale, and symbols for important landmarks.

Where did you hide your buried treasure?

PART III

The Land

From space, Earth looks like a big blue ball with patches of green and brown. Those patches of green and brown are the land we live on. Land covers 29 percent, or a little more than one-quarter, of the planet's surface. The rest is water.

The surface of Earth seems smooth and flat when seen from far away. But up close you can see the wide variety of landforms that make up the continents and other landmasses. **Plains, mountains, plateaus, hills, buttes, canyons, valleys,** and **basins** are the major landforms of our planet. The process of land formation goes on every day. Movements of the earth, such as earthquakes and volcanoes, weathering from wind and water, and the accumulation of sediments deposited as the result of erosion, are the main forces that shape the land. They build the land up, wear it down, and alter its surface. Sometimes these changes happen quickly, as in an earthquake, but more often they occur slowly over time.

The shape of the land affects how people live, work, and play. It influences the weather, how we get from place to place, the location of our towns and cities, the kinds of foods we grow, what we wear, and the design of our buildings. How does the landscape where you live influence your community?

17

The Continents

The biggest landmasses on Earth are the seven **continents**—North America, South America, Europe, Asia, Africa, Australia, and Antarctica. The word *continent* comes from a Latin word meaning "a continuous landform." In their definition of a continent, however, most geographers include both the large landmass and its associated islands. Greenland, for instance, is part of North America, and Indonesia is part of Asia. A few islands and island chains, including New Zealand, French Polynesia, Samoa, and Hawaii, are not part of any continent.

Altogether the continents total about 57 million square miles (148 million sq km) of land. Except for Europe and Asia, each continent is surrounded by water. Most geographers divide Europe and Asia along a line running from the northern Ural Mountains, south to the Caspian Sea, and west to the Dardanelles. Hundreds of

THE CONTINENTS

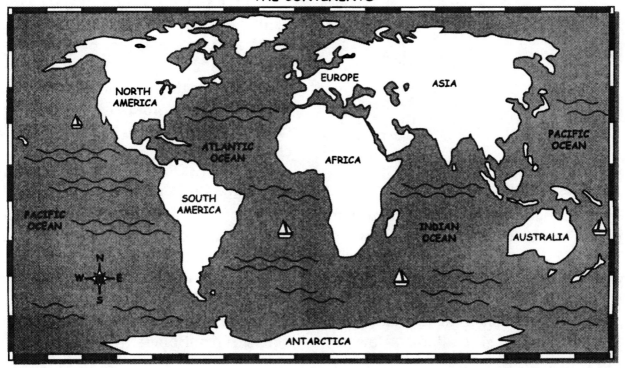

The city of the Istanbul in Turkey is in both Asia and Europe. If you go to Istanbul you can cross a bridge from one continent to the other. Look at a map of the world. Can you find some other places in the world where two continents are so close together that you could easily cross from one to the other?

Answer: Strait of Gibraltar, border of Panama and Colombia, Suez Canal.

millions of years ago the landmasses that are now Europe and Asia were separate. They merged about 240 million years ago, just before the time of the first dinosaurs.

Land Area of the Continents

Asia	17,176,094 sq mi (44,485,900 sq km)
Africa	11,687,183 sq mi (30,269,680 sq km)
North America	9,357,290 sq mi (24,235,280 sq km)
South America	6,880,635 sq mi (17,820,770 sq km)
Antarctica	5,100,000 sq mi (13,209,000 sq km
Europe	4,065,944 sq mi (10,530,750 sq km)
Australia	2,966,151 sq mi (7,682,300 sq km)

Earth's Crust

The continents are part of the hard outer layer of the Earth that is the Earth's crust. This rigid outer portion of the Earth ranges in thickness from less than 6 miles (10 km) to about 25 miles (42 km). The crust is thickest under the continents and thinnest under the seafloor. Below the

crust lies the mantle, a 1,800-mile- (3,000-km-) thick region of hot mineral matter. Earth's core, which is made of iron and nickel, consists of a liquid outer layer and a solid inner core.

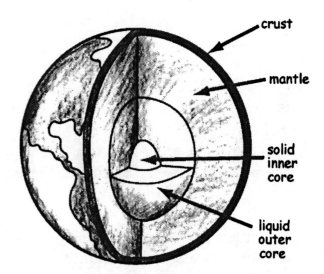

crust

mantle

solid inner core

liquid outer core

Cross-Section of Earth's Interior

On the surface of the Earth, the continents are slowly moving across the melted rock below. It is as if the continents were giant ships sliding on top of a fiery sea. Scientists call this movement **continental drift.** The positions of the continents on the Earth's surface are constantly changing.

Millions of years ago, the world looked very different from the way it looks today. Some of the continents were joined together and others were separate landmasses. Over time they have moved. Most of Earth's landmasses were in the southern hemisphere 480 million years ago. Today the landmasses are located mainly in the northern hemisphere.

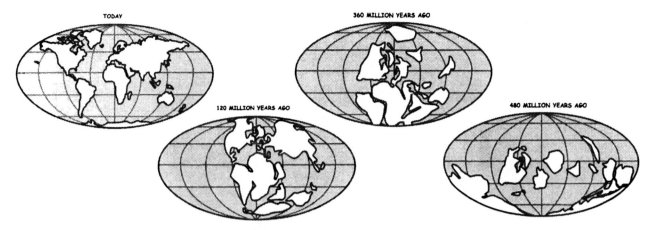

India was once a separate landmass. For that reason, it is sometimes called a subcontinent. Beginning about 120 million years ago, India slowly moved northward and eventually joined Asia, pushing up the Himalaya Mountains in the process. India is still pushing northward, and every year the mountains become a little bit higher—growing about 1 inch (2.5 cm) every five years.

2. Take the tracing paper off the map and cut out the shapes of the continents. Put them on a table. Push the pieces together until the continents almost bump into each other. Can you see how some of the continents might have been joined a long time ago?

MAP PUZZLE

You can make a map puzzle to see how some continents may have fit together a long time ago.

You will need:

scissors

tracing paper about 9 by 12 inches (23 by 30 cm)

map of the world, about 9 by 12 inches (23 by 30 cm)

2 paper clips

pencil

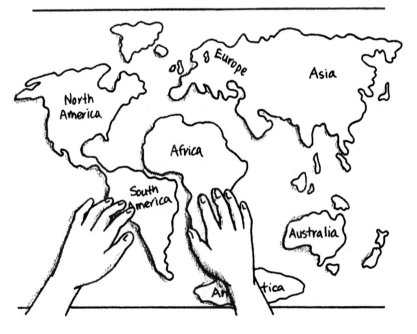

1. Cut the tracing paper to fit over the map of the world. Use the paper clips to hold the tracing paper in place. Using the marking pen, trace the shapes of the continents.

3. Take your puzzle pieces and line them up according to size. Which is the biggest? Which is the smallest? Use the chart of the land area of the continents to check your work.

18

Earthquakes

Even though we don't usually notice it, the Earth's crust is constantly moving. The study of how the continental plates move and connect is called **plate tectonics.** Sometimes two of Earth's plates crash into each other and push up huge mountains. This is how the Himalaya mountain range in Asia was formed. Sometimes a plate will break apart, forming a gap called a **rift,** such as the huge Rift Valley in East Africa. In other cases, when two plates meet, they just slide by each other like two giant ships at sea. Sometimes, instead of slipping past each other, two meeting plates get stuck. Then pressure builds up as the plates try to push past each other. When the pressure is great enough, they slip apart suddenly and create an **earthquake.**

Earthquakes are the most deadly of natural disasters and are responsible for almost 50 percent of twentieth-century calamities in which 10,000 or more people have died. The most destructive earthquake in the United States was in San Francisco in 1906. It destroyed much of the city and killed more than 500 people.

Although most earthquakes in the United States occur in Alaska and California, no state is immune to the threat of earthquakes. Since 1700, more than 1,000 earthquakes have been reported east of the Mississippi River. An earthquake in New Madrid, Missouri, in 1811, with an estimated Richter scale rating of 8.7, was the most powerful earthquake to have ever occurred in the lower 48 states.

THE RICHTER SCALE

The Richter scale was developed by an American scientist, Charles Richter, in 1935 to measure the amount of energy generated by an earthquake. Each unit on the scale is about 60 times greater than the previous one. An earthquake with a Richter rating of 7 is about 200,000 times as powerful as an earthquake with a Richter rating of 4. Usually it takes an earthquake of 6.5 or larger to cause major injuries to people and damage to property.

EARTHQUAKE
IN A BOX

You can make a tiny earthquake in a box. It is best to do this project outside.

You will need:
scissors
shallow box
damp, clean sand

1. Cut the box in half.

2. Put the box back together by slightly overlapping the cut edges.

3. Fill the box with sand and pat the sand with your hand to make it smooth. Now slowly push the two parts of the box together. What happened to the sand? Did it form any little hills or valleys? Did you make any earthquakes?

4. Smooth the sand again. Slowly pull the two halves of the box apart. What happened in the middle?

19

Volcanoes

A **volcano** is a vent, or opening, in the Earth's crust that allows molten lava, gases, and other materials to come out of the Earth's interior. (The word *volcano* comes from the name "Vulcan"; Vulcan was the ancient Roman god of fire.) The largest number of active volcanoes occurs in the lands at the edge of the Pacific Ocean, an area known as the Ring of Fire. The Ring of Fire marks the boundary where the geologic plates under the Pacific Ocean meet the plates that form the surrounding continents. Volcanoes also occur in places where plates pull apart and form rifts, as in Iceland, and where molten rock leaks up through "holes" in the Earth's crust, as in Hawaii.

Volcanoes are one way of building mountains. Material erupts from within the Earth, accumulating outside the vent and forming one of three basic shapes. The cinder cone volcano is a small, steep-sided, stubby-topped formation that consists mainly of cinders and ash. Parícutin,

MAJOR VOLCANOES OF THE WORLD

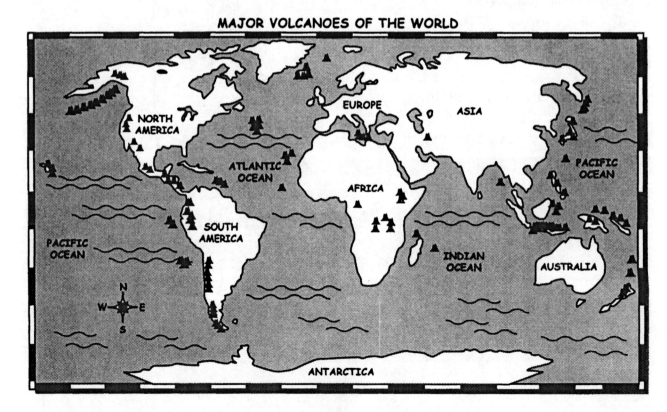

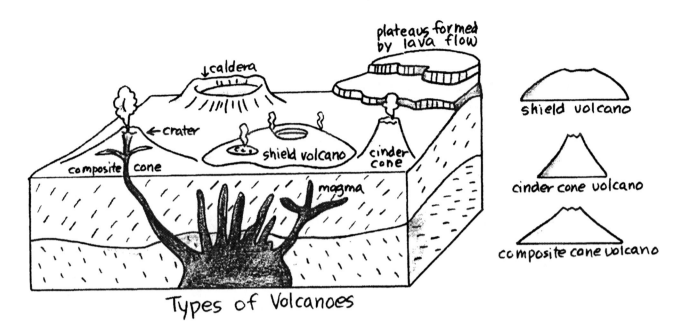

plateaus formed by lava flow

caldera

crater

composite cone

shield volcano

cinder cone

magma

shield volcano

cinder cone volcano

composite cone volcano

Types of Volcanoes

in Mexico, is an example of a cinder cone. Most of the world's major volcanoes have composite cones, made up of alternating layers of lava and fragments of other kinds of rocks. The sides are less steep than those of a cinder cone and the top is more pointed. Mount Fujiyama, in Japan, is a good example of a composite cone. A shield, or dome, volcano is a broad-based, gently sloping formation. It is built by a series of thin, widespread lava flows. Mauna Loa on the island of Hawaii is a shield volcano.

An extremely large crater at the top of the volcano is called a caldera. At Crater Lake National Park in California, the caldera of a volcano has filled with water to become a deep lake.

Volcanic eruptions can be extremely violent. The explosion of the Krakatau volcano in Indonesia in 1883 was heard 2,900 miles (4,700 km) away! Tidal waves, or **tsunamis,** resulting from that eruption killed 36,000 people and traveled around the world as far as England. Some

volcanoes are extremely active and erupt constantly, while others are inactive, or dormant, with many years between eruptions. Extinct volcanoes are those that have not erupted in historic times.

FROSTING LAVA

You can demonstrate how pressure forces lava through cracks in the Earth.

You will need:
tube of red frosting
nail
hammer

1. Poke a hole into the side of the frosting tube about ½ inch (1 cm) from the cap by pounding the nail lightly with the hammer.

2. Squeeze the tube from the bottom. Does frosting ooze out of the hole? In the same way, pressure forces hot lava up through holes in the Earth's crust.

3. Poke several more holes in the frosting tube next to your original hole to make a line. Squeeze the tube again. The series of frosting "eruptions" is something like a line of volcanoes along the Ring of Fire.

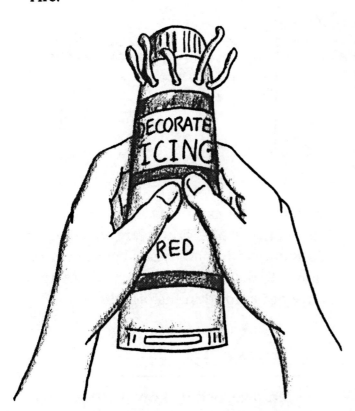

Some of the World's Active Volcanoes

Volcano	Location	Last Eruption
Erebus	Ross Island, Antarctica	1998
Fuji	Honshu, Japan	1708
Krakatau	Indonesia	2000
Pelée	Martinique	1932
Mauna Loa	Hawaii, Hawaii	1984
Kilauea	Hawaii, Hawaii	2000
Etna	Italy	2000
Vesuvius	Italy	1944
Stromboli	Italy	2000
Santorini	Greece	1950
Popocatepetl	Mexico	1999
Rainier	Washington	1894
Saint Helens	Washington	1991
Shasta	California	1786
Colima	Mexico	1999
El Chichon	Mexico	1982

MOUNT VESUVIUS

One of the world's most famous volcanic eruptions was at Mount Vesuvius in Italy in A.D. 79. The ancient Roman historian Pliny the Younger described the event, saying "A sudden and stupendous crash resounded, as if the whole mountain were caving in. Immense boulders flew up in the air as high as the crater edge. Then came a huge fire and so much smoke that the whole sky went dark and the sun entirely disappeared as if in an eclipse." When the eruption subsided, the ancient city of Pompeii was buried under 20 feet (6.2 m) of ash and mud, and lava had destroyed nearby Herculaneum, killing an estimated 20,000 people. Much of our knowledge of ancient Roman life comes from the archeological evidence buried at those two sites.

20

High Places and Low Places

Mountains are found on every continent and on the seafloor. Most geologists classify a **mountain** as land rising more than 1,000 feet (300 m) above the surrounding landscape. Most mountains of the world belong to one of three major systems of mountain ranges. One system lies along the western edges of North and South America. Another stretches across Europe and Asia. The third system includes peaks in Australia, the western Pacific, and eastern Asia. The highest mountains of all are the Himalayas in Asia. Some of their peaks are more than five miles (8.3 km) high.

The lowest land on Earth is the shore of the Dead Sea in Israel. It is 1,312 feet (400 m) below sea level. The Dead Sea lies in the bottom of a deep valley and is surrounded by steep cliffs and mountains.

Highest and Lowest Points of Each Continent

Continent	Highest Point	Lowest Point
Asia	Mount Everest (Nepal): 29,035 (8,850m)	Dead Sea shore (Israel): 1,312 feet (400 m) below sea level
Africa	Mount Kilimanjaro (Tanzania): 19,340 feet (5,895 m)	Lake Assal shore (Djibouti): 512 feet (156 m) below sea level
North America	Mount McKinley (Alaska): 20,320 feet (6,194 m)	Death Valley (California): 282 feet (86 m) below sea level
South America	Mount Aconcagua (Argentina): 23,034 feet (7,020 m)	Valdes Peninsula (Argentina): 131 feet (40 m) below sea level
Antarctica	Vinson Massif: 16,864 feet (5,140 m)	sea level
Europe	Mont Blanc (France): 15,771 feet (4,807 m)	sea level
Australia	Mount Kosciusko (New South Wales): 7,308 feet (2,249 m)	Lake Eyre shore (South Australia): 38 feet (11.7 m) below sea level

The sea is 47 miles (75 km) long, more than 9 miles (75 km) wide, and is almost 1,100 feet (331 m) deep. Its water is up to nine times saltier than ocean water.

MOUNTAINS OF THE WORLD

You can make a model of some of the world's tallest mountains.

You will need:

large plate, about 11 inches (28 cm) in diameter

7 sheets of brown or grey paper, about 9 inches by 12 inches (25 by 30 cm)

pen or pencil

small plate, about 8 inches (20 cm) in diameter

cup, about 3 inches (8 cm) in diameter

scissors

transparent tape

ruler

7 index cards

white paint (optional)

1. Lay the large plate upside down on a sheet of paper so that half of the plate covers the paper. Trace a line around the edge of the plate to make a half circle on the paper.

2. Lay the small plate on a sheet of paper and trace all around it to make a circle. Do this again on two more sheets of paper.

3. Put the cup on the last piece of paper and trace around it.

4. Cut out all the circles and the large half circle. Fold each circle in half and cut along the folded line. Now you have 1 large, 6 medium, and 2 small half circles. (One medium and one small half circle are extras.)

5. Hold the large half circle in two hands and bend it slightly at the center of the straight edge. Slide the two straight sides together to make a cone. Tape to hold. This cone will represent Mount Everest.

6. Make a tiny cone in the same way with one of the smallest half circles. This will be Mount Kosciusko.

7. Along the curved edge of four of the medium-size half circles, trim ¼ inch (0.5 cm), ½ inch (1.25 cm), ¾ inch (2 cm), and 1 inch (2.5 cm). You will have five different sizes with these and one of the untrimmed medium half circles. Make these into cones to represent the remaining five mountains: Mount Aconcagua, Mount McKinley, Mount Kilimanjaro, Vinson Massif, and Mont Blanc.

8. Arrange all the cones according to size from biggest to smallest. Fold each index card in half lengthwise and make a label for each mountain with its name and height. (See chart on page 51 for heights.)

9. You may want to paint the tops of your mountains white to represent snow. Your model is not perfectly to scale, but it will give you a good idea of how the sizes of the world's mountains compare.

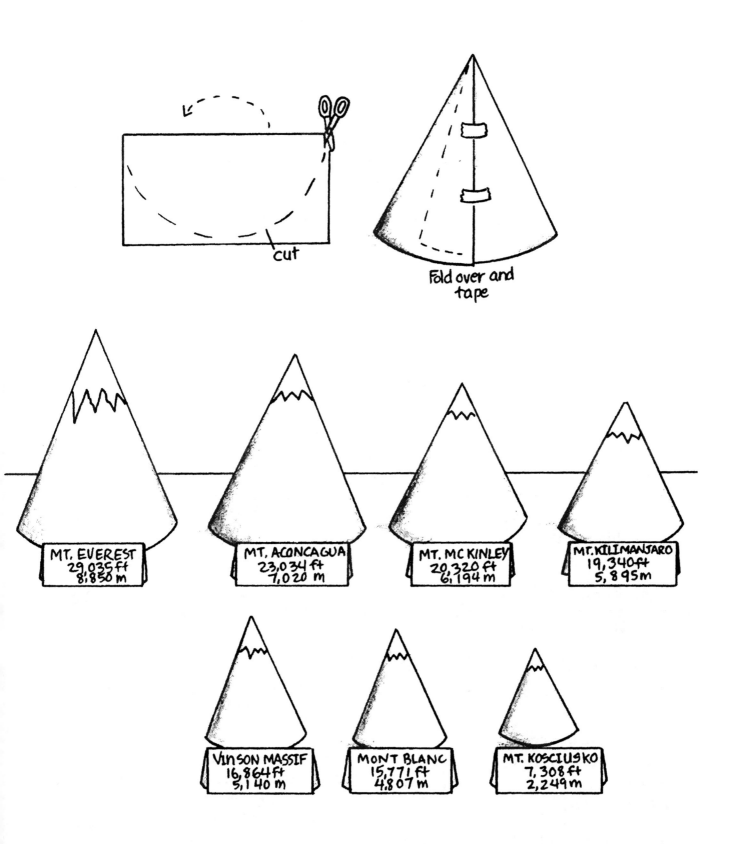

cut

Fold over and tape

MT. EVEREST
29,035 ft
8,850 m

MT. ACONCAGUA
23,034 ft
7,020 m

MT. MC KINLEY
20,320 ft
6,194 m

MT. KILIMANJARO
19,340 ft
5,895 m

VINSON MASSIF
16,864 ft
5,140 m

MONT BLANC
15,771 ft
4,807 m

MT. KOSCIUSKO
7,308 ft
2,249 m

21

How to Measure a Mountain

You can use a ruler or measuring tape to find out the height of small and medium-size objects. But for many things, such as tall buildings or trees, it is not practical to measure their height directly. Surveyors who map the land have sophisticated instruments for measuring the height of mountains and other large objects. Here is a simple way to estimate the height of a tall object such as a tree or a telephone pole.

HOW HIGH IS IT?

This project is easiest to do outdoors.

You will need:

sheet of newspaper
scissors
paper clips or transparent tape
small object (such as a stone) to use as a
  marker
measuring tape

1. Fold the newspaper into a triangle so that the two adjacent sides meet. Use the scissors to cut off the extra paper from the edge. Now fold the triangle in half again. Hold the four sheets together with paper clips or tape.

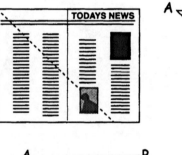

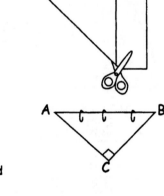

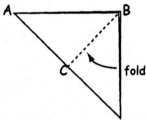

2. Turn the triangle so side C-B points to the sky and side A-C is parallel to the ground.

3. Find a tall object such as a tree. Stand far enough away from it so that you can see the top. Hold the newspaper up to your eye and look along the longest side of the triangle toward the top of the tree. The bottom of the newspaper triangle should point straight at the tree. Move

backward or forward as necessary so that the sloping side of the triangle (side A-B) points exactly to the top of the tree.

4. Using the stone, mark the spot where you are standing on the ground. Use the measuring tape to measure the distance between it and the tree. Add your height to that amount. The total distance will be about the same as the height of the tree. This method is not precise, but it is good for calculating the approximate height of objects too tall to measure directly.

Note: Look at the paper triangle. Can you see how two sides are the same length? If you know how long one side is, you also know how long the other side is. The same is true for measuring a big triangle of the same shape.

MEASURING THE EARTH

You may have seen workers looking around a building site or roadway using long poles and tripods mounted with instruments. They are surveyors. **Surveying** is the science of locating the position of points on the Earth's surface. Surveyors use a variety of instruments, including a compass for establishing direction, steel tape for measuring distance, poles or stakes as markers, a telescope with a level for establishing elevation, and a device called a transit that measures angles. These tools give surveyors the information they need to describe the shape of the land.

Topographic surveys provide maps of physical features such as mountains, plains, and rivers. Land surveys locate boundaries of land tracts and towns and cities. Other kinds of surveys chart the bottoms of lakes or the locations of rock formations and mineral resources.

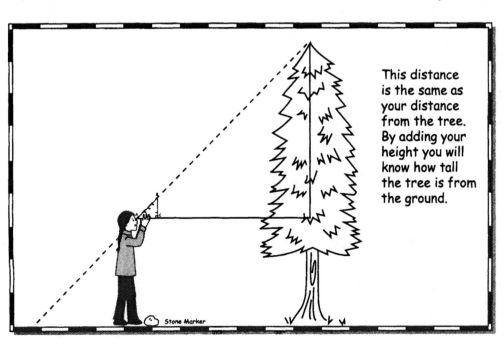

This distance is the same as your distance from the tree. By adding your height you will know how tall the tree is from the ground.

22

Valleys and Canyons

A **valley** is a long, natural depression in the Earth bordered by higher land. Valleys are found in high mountain ranges, in hills, in lowlands, and on the ocean floor. The movement of water, ice, or the Earth's crust leads to the formation and development of valleys. A **canyon** is a deep, narrow valley with steep sides. Canyons are also sometimes called gorges.

Valleys and canyons are formed when wind and/or water wears away, or erodes, the ground. The Grand Canyon of Arizona is an amazing example of **erosion**. There the Colorado River has worn away the earth and created a canyon over a mile (1.6 km) deep. The Grand Canyon has been forming for millions of years. Each layer of rock reveals a period in Earth's history. Rock erodes slowly, but soil or sand can erode quickly, especially if it is not protected from wind and water.

Human activity such as digging mines, damming rivers, cutting forests, and plowing fields increases the rate at which soil erodes. These kinds of activities remove the plants and trees whose roots anchor the soil and whose leaves and branches provide a protective cover for the ground.

When soil has no protection, a heavy rainstorm can create gullies as fast-flowing water washes away dirt. Building channels and sewers for water drainage are two ways of preventing soil erosion. Can you think of some others?

PREVENTING EROSION

You can do this erosion experiment outdoors in a sandbox or at a beach.

You will need:

sand

3-foot (1-meter) piece of rubber hose or flexible plastic tubing (you can get this at a hardware store)

bucket of water

funnel

1. Build two large sand hills. Bury the hose in one hill. One end of the hose should stick out of the top of the hill. The other end should stick out of the bottom.

2. Pour water onto the top of the hill without the hose. What happens as the water runs to the bottom? Does it wash away some of the sand?

3. Pour water through the funnel into the hose at the top of the other hill. Does the water come out the other end? How do you think that drainpipes and sewers help prevent erosion? Look for examples of erosion in your community.

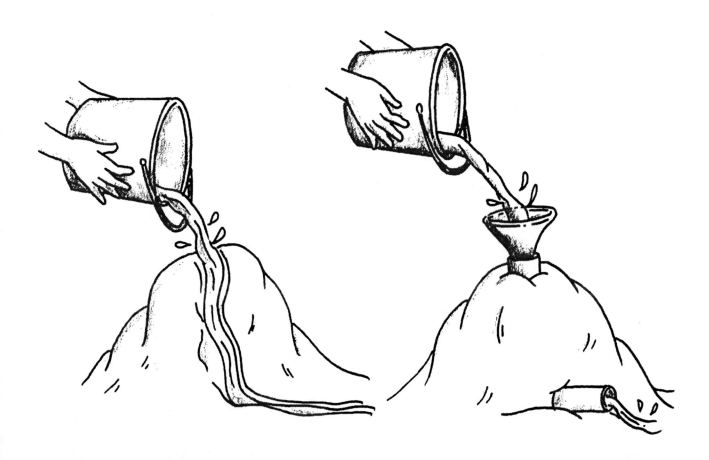

Where the Land Meets the Sea

Land with water all around it is an **island.** An island can be in the middle of a lake, a river, or an ocean. Australia is a continent that is also an island. So is Antarctica. The state of Hawaii has eight main islands and many small ones. The island of Manhattan is part of New York City. It is linked to other parts of the city by tunnels and bridges.

Island

A **peninsula** is like an island except that it is connected to land at one end. The word "peninsula" comes from two Latin words that mean "almost an island." The state of Florida is a peninsula. Its east

coast faces the Atlantic Ocean and its west coast faces the Gulf of Mexico.

Peninsula

Sometimes two large pieces of land are joined by a much smaller piece of land called an **isthmus.** The Isthmus of Panama joins North and South America. Until the Panama Canal was finished in 1914, ships sailing west from ports in the Atlantic to ports in the Pacific had to go around the southern tip of South America. Some of them sailed through the Strait of Magellan. A **strait** is a narrow passage of water that connects two larger bodies of water.

58

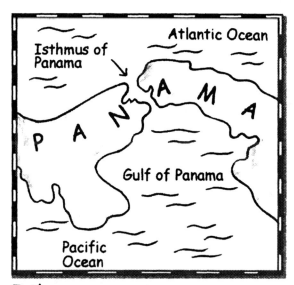

Isthmus

Strait

Bay

Fjord

A **bay** is a place where dry land partly encloses a small area of a sea or lake. Coves and inlets are very small bays. Large, deep bays are often used as harbors. Many of the world's cities have been built around harbors. San Francisco Bay in California is a huge harbor for vessels ranging from small pleasure boats to huge tanker ships.

A **fjord** is a long, narrow ocean inlet.

Fjords form in U-shape valleys that were carved by glaciers. These deep channels may be thousands of feet (meters) deep, and they usually have steep walls rising above the water's surface. Fjords are found mainly in Norway, Alaska, Chile, New Zealand, Canada, and Greenland. The tall sides of a fjord protect the water from wind and make the fjord a safe harbor for ships.

ISLANDS IN A TUB

You can make your own small islands, peninsulas, isthmuses, and straits in a dishpan. You also may make some bays, inlets, and fjords.

You will need:

sand
large rocks
dishpan or tub
small plastic figures (optional)
pail of water

1. Put the sand and rocks into the dishpan. Arrange them to look like a small landscape. You may want to put small figures on the rocks.

2. Slowly add water. Can you see the rocks become islands and peninsulas? Did you form any isthmuses or straits? The same thing happens when people build dams. Water behind the dam fills valleys and the tops of hills become islands and peninsulas. Sometimes the land becomes joined by small isthmuses or separated by narrow passages of water.

PART IV

Water All Around

Almost three-quarters of the Earth is covered with water. You can find water in oceans, seas, lakes, rivers, streams, canals, reservoirs, ponds, and swamps. Water also occurs in the form of rain, sleet, and snow and is found in large masses of ice called glaciers. In the atmosphere, water exists in a gaseous form as **water vapor.**

The total amount of water on Earth—including liquid water, ice, and water vapor—is about 336 million cubic miles (1.4 billion cubic km). Almost all of that, about 97 percent, is in the ocean.

24

Oceans, Seas, and Lakes

The **ocean** is the global expanse of water that surrounds the continents. Even though the ocean is continuous, geographers have given different names to parts of the ocean according to where it is separated by the continents and other landmasses. The main sections of the ocean in order of size are the Pacific, Atlantic, Indian, and Arctic oceans. The Pacific covers almost 65 million square miles (166 million sq km). It is both the biggest and deepest ocean. In some places it is over 6 miles (10 km) to the bottom!

A **lake** is a body of water surrounded by land. Lakes are found on every continent and vary greatly in size, from tiny

OCEANS OF THE WORLD

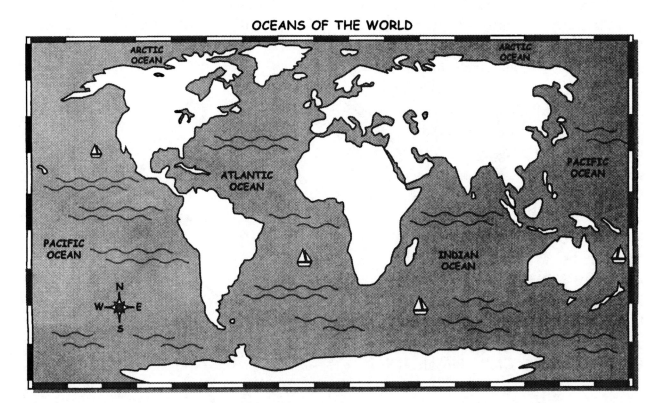

Water Areas of the Earth

Ocean or Sea	Area (in sq mi/sq km)
Pacific Ocean	64,186,300/166,241,700
Atlantic Ocean	33,420,000/82,522,600
Indian Ocean	28,350,500/73,342,660
Arctic Ocean	5,105,700/14,056,000
Caribbean Sea	971,400/2,512,300
Mediterranean Sea	969,100/2,509,700
Bering Sea	873,000/2,266,250
Gulf of Mexico	582,100/1,554,000
Sea of Okhotsk	537,500/1,528,100
Sea of Japan	391,100/1,007,500
Hudson Bay	281,900/822,300
East China Sea	256,600/664,800
Black Sea	196,100/479,150
Red Sea	174,900/437,700
North Sea	164,900/427,200
Baltic Sea	147,500/382,100
Remaining bodies of water	3,675,753/9,522,360

ponds to areas so large that they are called **seas.** Partially enclosed parts of the ocean are also sometimes called seas. The largest lake in the world is the Caspian Sea, on the border of Europe and Asia. It has an area of 143,240 square miles (371,000 sq km). The biggest lakes in the United States are the Great Lakes. In order of size they are Lake Superior, Lake Michigan, Lake Ontario, Lake Erie, and Lake Huron. (Here's a trick for remembering the names of the Great Lakes. The first letters can be arranged to spell the word "HOMES.")

Ocean and sea water is salty. Some lakes are also made of salt water, but most have **fresh water.** Great Salt Lake in Utah, the Salton Sea in California, and Lake Nakuru in Kenya are all salt lakes.

You may have swum in the ocean or a salt-water lake. Even though the water was clear, you would have been able to taste the salt on your tongue. When salt dissolves in water, it disappears. Here is an experiment you can do to make it reappear.

MAKING SALT CRYSTALS

You will need:

1 cup sea water (If you do not live near the ocean or a salt lake, you can make your own sea water by mixing 2 teaspoons table salt with 2 cups [.5 liter] water.)

pie pan

magnifying glass

1. Pour the sea water into the pan. Put the pan in a warm, dry place and let the water evaporate. (This will take a few

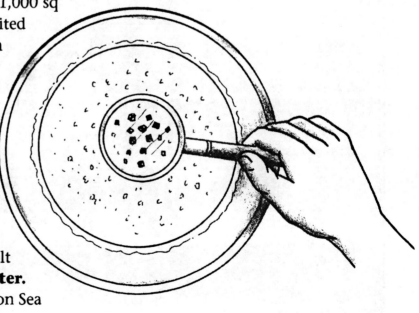

days.) What do you see when the water is all gone?

2. Look at the salt crystals with the magnifying glass. What shape are they? Each kind of mineral forms its own crystal shapes. Can you see the X-shape indentation on the top of each sodium chloride crystal?

About two-thirds of the salt that is dissolved in sea water is sodium chloride, or ordinary table salt. Other salts that occur in sea water include magnesium chloride, sodium sulfate, potassium chloride, and calcium chloride. There are also traces (extremely tiny amounts) of about 60 other elements. When water evaporates from the sea, the salt is left behind, just as it was in your salt crystal project. This means that the water vapor in the atmosphere, which falls back to Earth as rain, is fresh water.

25

Rivers and Streams

When rain falls on the land, it runs downhill. Little streams join bigger streams that flow into rivers. A **river** is a large natural stream of flowing water. Eventually most rivers empty into the ocean. If you are flying in an airplane and look out the window at the ground, often you can see these networks of waterways.

All rivers east of the Rocky Mountains eventually flow into the Atlantic Ocean. All rivers west of the Rocky Mountains flow into the Pacific Ocean. The Rocky Mountains form what is called the **continental divide.**

Rivers are among the most important natural features of the Earth. The earliest

River Systems

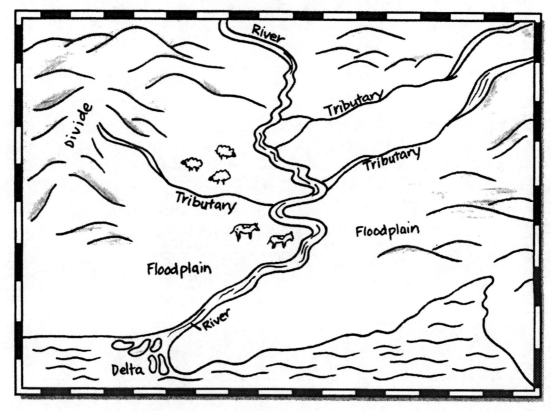

civilizations grew up along rivers, such as the Nile in Egypt, the Tigris and Euphrates in Mesopotamia, and the Indus in India. Rivers provided water for drinking and agriculture and were "roads" for transportation and trade. Today rivers are also sources of power for operating machines and generating electricity. Many of the world's great cities, such as London, New York, and Shanghai, have grown up along riverbanks. Can you think of some other cities that are on rivers?

How Does the Water Flow?

This project needs to be done in a sink or bathtub or outdoors.

You will need:

a board about 2 by 3 feet (.6 by 1 m) long (such as a large bread board or a piece of plywood)

pitcher of water

plasticene

1. Tilt the board so that one end goes into the sink and the other end is raised about 1 inch (2.5 cm).

2. Pour the water slowly onto the raised end of the board and watch it flow to the other end. Does it form a little river?

3. Raise the end of the board to about 3 inches (8 cm) and pour the water again. Raise it a little more and pour the water one more time. Does the water flow faster each time you raise the board? Why? What other differences do you notice in the water flow as the slant of the board becomes steeper?

4. Lay the board on a flat surface. Use the plasticene to create some small hills and mountain ranges on the board.

5. Raise the board and pour the water. How do the mountains of plasticene alter the course of your river?

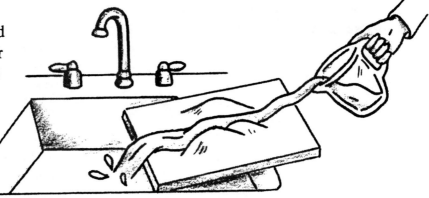

Longest Rivers of the World

River	Outflow	Length (miles/km)	Continent
Nile	Mediterranean	4,160/6,656	Africa
Amazon	Atlantic	4,000/6,400	South America
Chang	East China Sea	3,964/6,342	Asia
Huang	Yellow Sea	3,395/5,432	Asia
Ob-Irtish	Gulf of Ob	3,362/5,603	Asia
Congo	Atlantic Ocean	2,900/4,640	Africa
Lena	Laptev Sea	2,734/4,374	Asia
Mekong	South China Sea	2,700/4,320	Asia
Niger	Gulf of Guinea	2,590/4,144	Africa
Parana	Rio de la Plata	2,485/3,976	South America

THE MIGHTY MISSISSIPPI

The Mississippi River is the longest river in the United States. It begins as a stream flowing out of Lake Itasca in Minnesota and flows 2,348 miles (3,757 km) to New Orleans. There it fans out into the broad Mississippi Delta and flows into the Gulf of Mexico. Throughout American history the Mississippi River has been an important transportation route carrying people and goods to ports along the water's edge. The American writer Mark Twain (Samuel Clemens) based his book *Huckleberry Finn* on his boyhood experiences in Hannibal, Missouri, a town on the banks of the Mississippi.

DELTAS

A **delta** is a fan-shape deposit that sometimes forms at the mouth of a river. Deltas form when a river flows into a quiet body of water such as a lake, gulf, or inland sea. As the river slows down, it drops the sediment that it was carrying from upstream. The heavier, coarser material settles first, and the smaller particles are carried farther downstream, sometimes beyond the mouth of the river. As the sediment builds up, new land is formed, often in the shape of a triangle. (The shape of the Greek letter "delta" is a triangle.) The Mississippi River carries more than 200 million tons of sediment each year into the Gulf of Mexico, and its delta is constantly growing. But not all rivers build deltas. The Columbia River in the Pacific Northwest, for instance, does not have a delta because the ocean currents at its mouth are so strong they carry away the sediment before it has a chance to accumulate.

26

Waterfalls, Rapids, and Other Fast Water

Rivers are a powerful force in shaping the land. They carve out valleys, slopes, and cliffs by erosion. As tiny bits of earth are worn away, they become suspended in the water and carried downstream. Each year rivers carry away about 22 billion tons of rocks, soil, and sand from the land and dump it into seas and lakes.

As water in rivers and streams goes downhill on its way to the sea, it often forms rapids and waterfalls. A **waterfall** is a steep descent of a river over a rocky ledge. The world's tallest waterfall is Angel Falls in Venezuela, which drops 3,212 feet (979 m) over a cliff into the Amazon rain forest. One of the world's widest waterfalls is also in South America. It is a series of falls on the Iguacu River that stretch more than 2 miles (3 km) between Brazil and Argentina.

When the force of falling water is strong enough, it can be used to move water turbines or water wheels. Water turbines are enclosed fan- or propellerlike devices that turn as water passes through them. They can be used to turn large gen-erators to produce electric power. Water wheels are among the oldest machines in the world. They have been used for many centuries to operate machinery such as saws or grinding wheels. You can make a small water wheel to see how it works.

WATER WHEEL

You will need:

ruler

pencil

lightweight cardboard about 8 by 10 inches (20 by 25 cm)

cup

scissors

white glue

empty thread spool

transparent tape

string about 12 inches (30 cm) long

sink faucet

1. Use the ruler to draw five squares on the cardboard 1¼ inches (3.5 cm) on each side.

2. Trace around the cup to make a circle on the cardboard.

3. Cut out the circle and the squares.

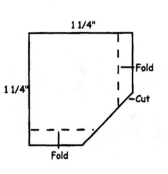

4. Cut one corner off each square, as shown. Fold back the two short sides ¼ inch (.5 cm) from the edge.

5. Using the point of the scissors, cut a small hole in the center of the circle. Draw five evenly spaced lines to the edge, like the spokes of a wheel.

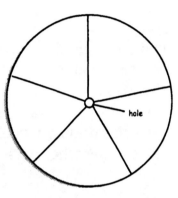

6. Glue the spool to the center of the cardboard circle. Make sure that the hole is lined up with the hole in the cardboard.

7. One at a time, place a square on a spoke of the circle. Tape one folded edge to the circle and one folded edge to the spool, as shown. When you are finished, it will look like a tiny water wheel.

8. Put the string through the hole. When you hold each end of the

string and pull it tight, the water wheel should spin.

9. Turn on the water at a faucet in a sink. Hold the water wheel under the flowing water and watch it spin.

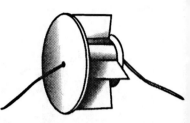

Does it spin faster at the top of the stream of water or at the bottom? Where do you think the water is more powerful?

NIAGARA FALLS

The Niagara River, which connects Lake Erie and Lake Ontario, has two waterfalls, one in New York State that is 193 feet (59 m) high and the other in Ontario, Canada, that is 186 feet (57 m) high. Together they are more than ½ mile (0.8 km) wide. Up to 195,000 cubic feet (5,525 cubic m) of water flow over Niagara Falls each second! That water is used to generate power that is used in both the United States and Canada.

27

Hit the Beach

Over time, flowing rivers and pounding ocean waves can grind even the mightiest rocks into sand. Sand is a tiny particle of a rock or mineral or of some other hard material, such as coral. Geologists define sand as any particle between .0025 inch and .079 inch in diameter, a size that is just large enough to see with the human eye.

Different kinds of rock make different sizes and colors of sand. Most sand consists of quartz, a semiclear rock, but other minerals such as feldspar, mica, magnetite, and garnet are often mixed with the quartz give the sand its particular color. The sands of White Sands National Monument in New Mexico are pure gypsum. Some beaches in Hawaii are black because the sand is made of tiny bits of hardened black lava. Beaches in Florida and the Caribbean are white because they are made of tiny bits of calcium carbonate from crushed coral and shells.

A SAND COLLECTION

You can collect different kinds of sand and display your collection in small bottles. Try to find out what kind of minerals make up your sand. Note any other objects in the sand, such as small rocks and shells. Label each bottle with the date and place where you found the sand and any other information you have about it.

SAND PICTURES

You will need:

old newspapers
crayons or markers
colored construction paper
white glue
sand

1. Spread out the newspapers where you will work.

2. Using crayons or markers, draw a picture on the colored paper, leaving portions that you will fill with sand.

3. Spread glue in each place where you want the sand to stick. Sprinkle sand over the picture so that it sticks to the glue. Shake the extra sand off the picture and onto the newspaper. The sand on the drawing will give your picture a rough texture and create the impression of a real beach or real rocks.

71

4. You may want to add other objects, such as shells, sticks, or seeds, to make your picture even more realistic.

28

Dams and Reservoirs

A dam is a strong, thick wall built across a river valley. In some cases dams are thick banks of earth. In other cases they are constructed of cement and steel. Water flowing over or through the dam often is used to generate electricity. The lake that forms behind the dam is a **reservoir.**

Sometimes too much rain falls and a flood occurs. Sometimes too little rain falls and there is a **drought.** Dams and reservoirs help prevent floods by controlling the water flow. Water can be released a little at a time from the dam so that it does not overflow the banks of the river. Reservoirs are also important for saving water to use in times of drought.

The Hoover Dam on the Colorado River in Nevada provides water and power to people in Arizona, Nevada, and southern California. Constructed of concrete, it is 726 feet (221 m) high and 660 feet (201 m) thick at the base. Its reservoir, Lake Mead, which can hold more than 29 million acre-feet (35 billion cubic meters) of water, is the largest in the United States. Other large dams in the United States include the Oroville Dam in California, the Glen Canyon Dam in Colorado, and the Garrison Dam in North Dakota.

BUILDING A BETTER DAM

You will need:

scissors
poster board
rectangular fish tank
plasticene
pencil
ruler
strip of paper about 1 inch (2.5 cm) wide
transparent tape
pitcher of water

1. Cut a piece of poster board so that it is about 10 inches (25 cm) high and ½ inch (1 cm) wider than the width of the tank.

2. Cut another piece of poster board that is twice the width of the tank. Set it aside.

3. Place the first piece of poster board in the tank so the edges meet the sides. The poster board will curve slightly. Press the plasticene along the edges of the poster board and the sides and bottom of the tank to make a watertight seal.

4. Use the pencil and ruler to mark lines 1 inch (2.5 cm) apart on the strip of paper. Tape the paper to the outside of the tank as shown.

73

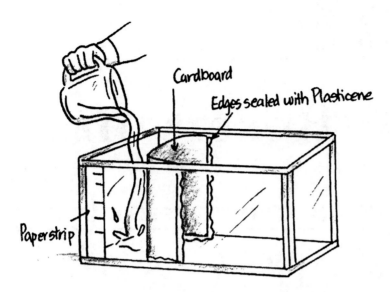

Cardboard

Edges sealed with Plasticene

Paperstrip

5. Slowly pour water into the tank in front of the dam as shown. Look at the lines on the paper strip to measure the water level. At what point does the poster board dam collapse from the pressure of the water?

6. Repeat the experiment with the larger piece of poster board. This piece of poster board will have to curve much more to fit in the tank. How much water does this dam hold? What is one way that engineers can make dams stronger?

THE JOHNSTOWN FLOOD

Johnstown is a small city in western Pennsylvania built on the floodplain where the Little Conemaugh and Stony rivers meet. In the late 1800s a small resort community grew up 14 miles (22.5 km) upriver from the town around a lake that had been created by damming the Little Conemaugh with a large earthen dam. The South Fork Dam was poorly maintained, and everyone worried that it might not hold in a heavy rain. On May 31, 1889, everyone's fears were realized. Spring rains had swollen the rivers and lakes beyond capacity. Suddenly, after a night of heavy downpours, a roar like thunder filled the air, and water burst through the dam. As it sped down the narrow valley toward the town, the muddy water destroyed everything in its path. More than 2,209 people died in the nation's worst flooding disaster. Today the remains of the South Fork Dam are part of a national park that is a memorial to the victims of the Johnstown Flood.

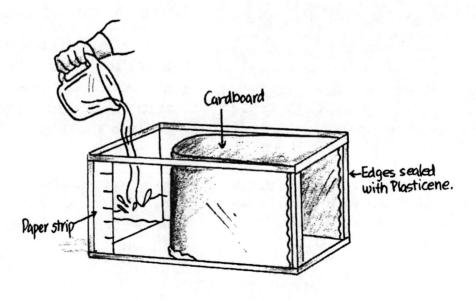

Cardboard

←Edges sealed with Plasticene.

Paper strip

29

The Water Cycle

Water moves constantly between the oceans and other bodies of water, the atmosphere, and the land. This is called the **water cycle.**

As the Sun warms the Earth, its heat causes water to evaporate from the land and the sea. Water vapor is also produced by plants and by people and animals. As water vapor rises in the atmosphere, it cools and often condenses to form clouds. Rain, snow, hail, or sleet may form in the clouds and then fall back to Earth. Any form of water that falls to Earth from the atmosphere is called **precipitation.**

Some of the water that falls on land flows along the surface of the ground into rivers, which eventually carry it back to the ocean. Another part of the water that falls as precipitation is absorbed by the soil. Some water in the soil evaporates, some is used by plants, and some seeps down to become **groundwater.** Groundwater is the accumulation of water stored in sand, gravel, porous rocks, and underground cavities. Groundwater feeds springs, wells, lakes, rivers, and the ocean. It is the main source of fresh water used by people.

Water Cycle

75

The upper portion of the water stored in the ground is called the **water table.** The water table generally follows the slope of the land above it, and in some cases it flows out onto the land surface, forming a pond, lake, or river. The depth of the water table changes from season to season and from year to year, depending on the amount of rain the area receives.

The total amount of water on Earth probably has remained the same since the oceans were formed. In other words, we are using the same water today as the dinosaurs drank hundreds of millions of years ago.

How Much Rain?

Rain forms as tiny droplets of water vapor combine to make bigger drops. Rain falls from clouds when these drops are 0.5 millimeter (.02 in) in diameter or larger. Drops smaller than that are called drizzle. Raindrops are more than a million times larger than the cloud droplets that formed them.

Rainiest Cities on Earth

City	Yearly Rainfall (inches/cm)
Bombay, India	85.4/225
Singapore	84.6/215
San Salvador, El Salvador	68.3/173
Lagos, Nigeria	59.3/151
Bangkok, Thailand	59.0/156
São Paulo, Brazil	57.4/152
Tokyo, Japan	55.4/141
Manila, Philippines	49.6/126
Auckland, New Zealand	49.4/125
Havana, Cuba	46.9/119
Sydney, Australia	46.4/118
Buenos Aires, Argentina	45.2/115
Shanghai, China	43.8/111

Each day more than 130 quadrillion gallons (491 quadrillion liters) of rain fall to Earth. If that rain were spread evenly over the planet, it would be 38 inches (almost 1 m) deep. But rain does not fall evenly. Some parts of the world have lots of rain, while others have very little. In most places the amount of rain varies from month to month.

MAKE A RAIN GAUGE

How much does it rain where you live? You can make a rain gauge to find out.

You will need:

masking tape about 1" wide

tall thin jar (an olive jar is good)

ruler

empty can with a wide opening (such as a tomato can)

pitcher of water

waterproof marking pen

1. Stick a strip of masking tape onto the tall thin jar from bottom to top.

2. Hold the ruler upright in the can. Pour water into the can until it measures ¼ inch (0.5 cm). Pour the water from the can into the jar and mark the level on the tape. Label it ¼ inch (0.5 cm). Pour the water out of the jar.

3. Hold the ruler in the can again and pour water into the can until it reaches ½ inch (1.25 cm). Pour this water into the jar, mark it, and write ½ inch (1.25 cm) on the tape. Repeat this for amounts of ¾ inch (2 cm), 1 inch (2.5 cm), and 2 inches (5 cm).

4. The jar is your rain gauge. The can is your rain collector. Put the can in an open space outdoors. After a rainstorm, pour the water from the can into the jar. By looking at the marks you made on the tape, you can see how much rain has fallen.

5. Why is it easier to measure the water in the jar? After a very heavy rainstorm, you may be able to measure the water directly in the large can with a ruler. But most storms produce less than 1 inch (2.5 cm) of rain. Then the small jar gives a more accurate measurement.

rain collector

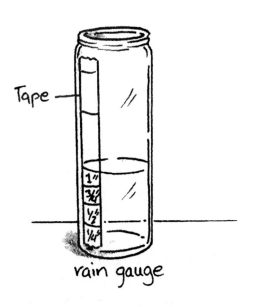

rain gauge

THE DRIEST PLACES ON EARTH

The Atacama Desert in Chile receives less than .02 inch (0.5 cm) of rainfall a year! It is the driest place on Earth. A **desert** is any place that receives less than 10 inches (25 cm) of annual rainfall. Desert regions of the Earth include parts of southern Australia, much of central Asia, northern Africa, parts of the southwestern United States, and Antarctica. We don't usually think of Antarctica as a desert because much of it is covered in ice, but it actually receives only a small amount of precipitation each year.

30

Glaciers, Ice Sheets, and Icebergs

Glaciers are huge pieces of ice that move slowly over land. They form in places where more snow piles up each year than melts. As new snow covers snow already on the ground, it presses down on the old snow. The old snow is compacted and turns into ice. When the ice becomes very thick—about 160 feet (50 m)—it is so heavy that it begins to slide downhill slowly. It becomes a river of frozen water. As it moves, it pulls along rocks and dirt, changing the land underneath.

An **ice sheet** is a broad layer of glacial ice that covers a large area. The Greenland ice sheet covers 670,000 square miles (1.7 million sq km) and is about 2 miles (3 km) thick at the center. Earth's other large ice sheet covers much of Antarctica. It contains about 85 percent of all the world's ice and about two-thirds of the world's fresh water.

When a large piece of ice breaks off the edge of a glacier and falls into the ocean, a process called calving, the chunks of floating ice are called **icebergs.** In the northern hemisphere, most icebergs break off glaciers in Greenland into the North Atlantic. Icebergs also form off the coast of Alaska in the Pacific. In the southern hemisphere, an iceberg the size of the state of Rhode Island recently broke off from Antarctica. Icebergs drift on ocean currents until they melt.

DANGER! ICEBERGS AHEAD!

When ice floats, about one-eighth of it sticks up above the surface of the water. The rest lies hidden below. That's why icebergs in the ocean are so dangerous. A ship may not see an iceberg until it is too late to avoid it. The sinking of the ocean liner *Titanic* in 1912 occurred after the ship ran into an iceberg, which tore a large hole in the ship's hull. More than 1,200 people died. Today an international iceberg patrol keeps track of icebergs in the North Atlantic in order to prevent such accidents from happening again.

In recent years, the average air temperature of Earth has been going up, and the polar ice sheets have begun to melt. If melting ice causes the sea level to go up by even a few feet, the chance of flooding for coastal cities could increase. Which cities in the United States could be affected by a sea level rise?

ICEBERGS AND SEA LEVEL

Do you think melting icebergs raise the sea level? Do this experiment and find out.

You will need:

glass bowl
water
ruler
ice cubes

1. Pour water into the bowl until it is about half full. Use the ruler to measure the height of the water.

2. Add the ice cubes. Measure the water level again. How much did it rise? Each ice cube is like a tiny iceberg.

3. Set the bowl in a warm place until all the ice is melted. Measure the water level again. What happened? (Remember that water increases in volume when it freezes.)

THE ICE AGES

An ice age is a very long period of cold climate during which glaciers cover large parts of Earth's surface. Scientists think that the Earth has had at least four ice ages. Ice is a powerful force in shaping the land. The most recent ice age, called the Pleistocene Epoch, began about 1.8 million years ago and lasted until about 10,000 years ago. So much of Earth's water was frozen then that at times the sea level was nearly 300 feet (100 m) lower than it is today and a land bridge connected what is now Siberia and Alaska. Humans came to North America from Asia across this land bridge, perhaps as early as 30,000 years ago.

The huge ice sheets of the Pleistocene carved much of the landscape of Canada and the northern United States. Advancing as far south as the state of Missouri, the moving ice scoured the land, carrying huge amounts of rock and soil from northern regions to places farther south. When the glaciers melted, they left behind depressions in the ground that filled with water and became lakes. Many of Minnesota's 10,000 lakes were created by glaciers of the Pleistocene.

PART V

Weather and Climate

Earth is surrounded by a thick, invisible layer made up of a mixture of gases, water vapor, and dust. This layer is Earth's **atmosphere.** It acts as a giant blanket, or insulator, and keeps the temperature of the planet's surface from becoming too hot or too cold.

Life on Earth could not exist without the atmosphere. The lower portion of the atmosphere contains the oxygen required by all land animals and many land plants. The atmosphere also protects living organisms from harmful radiation of the Sun, including most ultraviolet rays.

The atmosphere is where Earth's weather occurs. **Weather** refers to the conditions of the atmosphere at a particular time and place. It usually changes from hour to hour and day to day. Over many years, certain conditions are characteristic of the weather in an area. The average weather in an area, as well as its variations and extremes over many years, is called **climate.** Like weather, climate can change, but this happens much more slowly. What kind of weather and climate do you have where you live?

31

Atmospheric Pressure

Most of the time we don't notice the air around us. We can't see it, feel it, or smell it. Yet air takes up space and has its own weight and properties.

The weight of Earth's atmosphere overhead is called **atmospheric pressure.** We measure atmospheric pressure with a **barometer,** a device usually made from a glass tube and liquid mercury. The level of the mercury rises and falls with changes in pressure. The average pressure at sea level is about 29.9 inches (75.9 cm). Atmospheric pressure is reduced as altitude increases and with changes in weather.

Forecasters use their knowledge of pressure systems and changes in temperature and wind patterns to predict the weather. In a typical low-pressure weather system, the barometer measures about 29.4 inches (74.6 cm). Low pressure usually means rain. A typical high-pressure system measures about 30.4 inches (77.2 cm) and usually indicates a period of fair weather. Fast-moving streams of air in the upper atmosphere, called **jet streams,** move pressure systems around the world.

At sea level, the atmosphere exerts a pressure of 14.7 pounds (32.3 kg) per square inch (6.5 sq cm) on everything,

JET STREAMS

Jet streams are currents of eastwardly moving air about 5 to 9 miles (8 to 15 km) above the Earth. They form where large temperature differences occur in the atmosphere. They are faster in winter because air temperature differences are greater then. In winter the jet streams may blow at speeds more than 100 miles per hour (160 kph) whereas in summer they blow at about 50 mph (80 kph). Most of the time there are two jet streams in the northern and southern hemispheres—a subtropical current and another at the point where polar and temperate air meet. During the summer in the northern hemisphere, a high-altitude tropical jet stream moves in a westerly direction.

including our bodies. Atmospheric pressure decreases as you go higher in Earth's atmosphere. The pressure is reduced because there are fewer and fewer molecules of gas in the atmosphere and they are spaced farther apart. Less air and fewer gases means that there is less pressure. On top of Mount Everest the atmospheric pressure is only about 5 pounds (11 kg) per square inch (6.5 sq cm).

COLLAPSING BOTTLE

You will need:

about ½ cup (.25 liter) hot water
plastic drink bottle, 16.9 ounce (.5 liter)

1. Pour the hot water into the bottle. Screw the top on tightly.

2. Wait for the water to cool. (You can put it in a refrigerator so it will cool faster.)

3. Watch the bottle to see what happens. Molecules of hot air are spaced farther apart than those of cool air. As the air in the bottle cools, it takes up less space. In a few minutes the bottle will collapse. The atmospheric pressure of the outside air pushed the bottle in because it was stronger than the pressure inside the bottle.

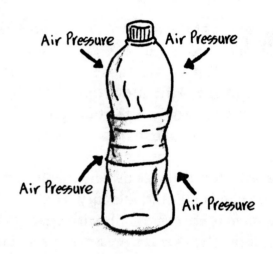

32

The Sun Keeps Us Warm

Because the Earth is round, the Sun heats it unevenly. The Sun's rays are strongest when they are directly overhead. Places near the equator get two and one-half times as much heat as the North and South poles, where the Sun's rays are always slanted.

ANGLE OF THE SUN

You can do a simple demonstration to see how the amount of light varies as the angle between the Earth and the Sun changes.

You will need:

flashlight   pencil
sheet of paper

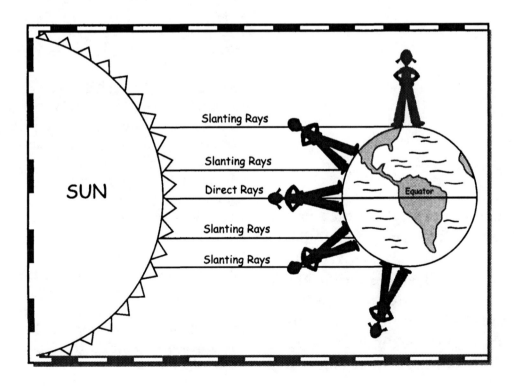

1. Hold the flash-light directly above the paper. The light should form a circle. Draw a line around the circle of light.

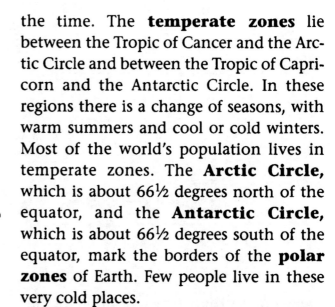
Direct ray

2. Move the flash-light so that it is about the same distance from the paper but at an angle. What has happened to the circle of light? In the same way, the Sun's rays are less strong when they shine at an angle because they spread out over a greater area on the Earth's surface.

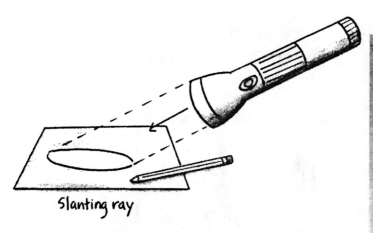
Slanting ray

Climate Zones

Earth is divided into climate zones according to the amounts of sunlight each part receives. The **tropical zone** of Earth lies between the **Tropic of Capricorn,** which is about 23½ degrees south of the equator, and the **Tropic of Cancer,** which is about 23½ degrees north of the equator. In this region the sunlight is most direct and the weather is warm much of the time. The **temperate zones** lie between the Tropic of Cancer and the Arctic Circle and between the Tropic of Capricorn and the Antarctic Circle. In these regions there is a change of seasons, with warm summers and cool or cold winters. Most of the world's population lives in temperate zones. The **Arctic Circle,** which is about 66½ degrees north of the equator, and the **Antarctic Circle,** which is about 66½ degrees south of the equator, mark the borders of the **polar zones** of Earth. Few people live in these very cold places.

Most of the United States is in the temperate zone. What part lies in the tropical zone? What part lies in the polar zone? Where do you live?

THE SEASONS

Because of Earth's tilted axis, we experience a change of seasons during Earth's 365-day revolution around the Sun. Summer occurs as the axis tilts toward the Sun, allowing more direct rays to hit Earth's surface; winter occurs as the axis tilts way from the Sun. The northern and southern hemispheres have opposite seasons, with the northern hemisphere having summer during the southern hemisphere's winter and winter during the southern hemisphere's summer. Spring and fall also occur at opposite times of year. The seasons change more dramatically as you move closer to the poles. In winter there is no sunlight at all in the polar zones while in summer the Sun shines around the clock. That's why the northern parts of Scandinavia are called the Land of the Midnight Sun. In the tropical zones of the world there are few seasonal differences.

33

Energy from the Sun

We could not live without energy from the Sun. Huge amounts of energy are created in the Sun's core as particles of hydrogen gas collide and fuse. That energy, in the form of heat and light, travels through space to Earth, where it provides warmth, causes wind and weather, and supports plant and animal life.

People can use the Sun's energy as an alternative to fossil fuels. A **passive solar energy system** is one that relies on natural methods of collecting and distributing heat from the Sun. Sunlight shining through windows into a house and warming the air inside is an example of passive solar energy. Which way should your house face to make the best use of this kind of solar energy?

An **active solar energy system** collects heat from the Sun and circulates it through a hot water or heating system. Some people put panels with special fluid-filled tubes on the roofs of their houses. Those panels collect the Sun's heat and are part of an active solar energy system. The hot fluid then circulates in pipes through the house, where it is used to heat water or warm the air. Solar panels also can contain **photovoltaic cells,** which convert the

Sun's energy into electricity. Sun-activated batteries provide power for machines ranging from calculators to satellites in space.

You can make a small solar water heater to learn how the Sun's rays can be used to make water warm.

SOLAR WATER HEATER

You will need:

black latex paint
paintbrush
aluminum pie plate
paper cup
water
thermometer
plastic wrap
masking tape
newspapers

1. Paint the inside of the pie plate with black paint and let it dry.

2. Fill the paper cup with cool water. Use the thermometer to measure the temperature of the water. Pour the water into the pie plate.

87

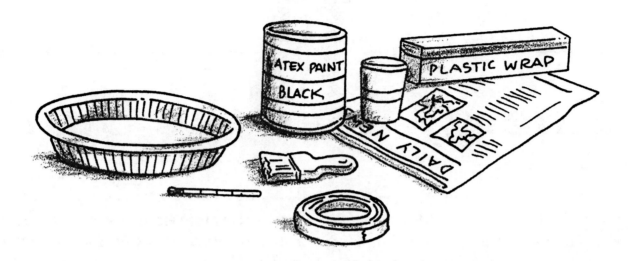

3. Cover the pie plate with plastic wrap and tape it in place.

4. Put the pie plate on a stack of newspapers in the sun.

5. Wait for 10 minutes. Then pour the water from the pie plate into the cup.

6. Measure the temperature of the water again. How much did the Sun heat the water?

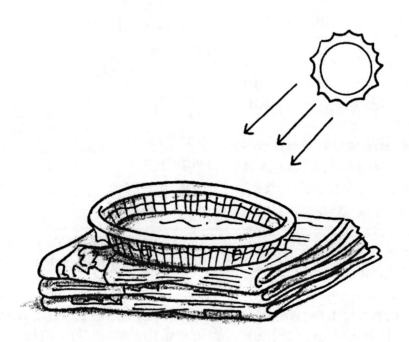

34

The Greenhouse Effect

The atmosphere is like a giant greenhouse over the Earth. A greenhouse is a building made of glass that's used for growing plants. The glass allows the Sun's rays to enter the greenhouse and keeps the warm air inside. The atmosphere is a window that lets in the Sun's rays so they can warm the surface of the planet. Some of the heat is absorbed by the land and water. Some of the heat is radiated, or reflected, back into the air. In the same way that the glass roof of a greenhouse prevents warm air from escaping, gases in the lower layer of the atmosphere trap much of Earth's radiated heat and prevent it from going into space. The warming of the atmosphere through heat absorption is known as the **greenhouse effect.**

MINI-GREENHOUSE

A block-and-board greenhouse is easy to assemble and works well for raising seedlings in small pots or milk cartons. Supplies for this project can be found at a hardware or garden store.

You will need:

5 wooden boards cut to 8 inches (20 cm) wide and about 3 feet (1 m) long

8 square concrete blocks, 8" by 8"

scissors

thick plastic sheeting about 3 feet (39 cm) wide and 10 feet (3 m) long

pushpins or thumbtacks

wood lath 3 feet (1 m) long (lath is a thin strip of wood)

small potted plants

Note: Construct outdoors in a sunny location.

1. Stack the boards and blocks together to make four shelves as shown on page 90.

2. Cut a piece of the plastic sheeting to cover the back and sides of the shelves. Fasten the plastic sheeting to the shelves with tacks.

3. Cut another plastic sheet to fit the front and fasten it to the top shelf so that it hangs down. Tack the lath to the bottom of the plastic. This will add weight to the plastic and keep it from flapping in the wind.

—plastic sheet

—square concrete blocks

—wood lath

4. Place the plants on the shelves.

5. On a sunny day, put your hand inside the plastic to feel the temperature of the air in the mini-greenhouse. How does it compare to the air outside?

GREENHOUSE GASES AND GLOBAL WARMING

The burning of coal, oil, gas, and other fossil fuels releases carbon dioxide, methane, and water vapor into the atmosphere. These "greenhouse gases" are responsible for trapping heat in the atmosphere. Many scientists think that the increase in the use of fossil fuels in the past century, which has resulted in an increased amount of these gases, has been one of the main reasons for the rise of the Earth's temperature, what has been called global warming. The Earth's temperature has been steadily increasing over the past 150 years, and scientists are predicting that it may increase by 11 degrees Fahrenheit (6 degrees Celsius) by the end of the century. How would a warmer climate change the planet?

35

Rising Air

When air is heated, it becomes lighter and rises. Have you ever watched a bird circle high into the air on outstretched wings? With almost no effort it may go up thousands of feet in a matter of minutes. The bird is catching an upward current of warm air called a **thermal.** Thermals form over portions of the land heated by the sun. Glider pilots and hang gliders also use thermals to gain altitude in the air.

In the same way that thermals are formed by the Sun heating the Earth, hot air rises above radiators and heating vents in our homes. You can see the effect of this rising air with a paper-plate snake.

TWIRLING SNAKE

You will need:

pencil

white paper plate (If you don't have a paper plate, you can trace around a dinner plate on a piece of heavy paper to make a circle and then cut it out.)

scissors

crayons or markers

heavy thread or thin string

1. Draw a spiral line on the paper plate, as shown. Keep the lines about 1 inch (2.5 cm) apart. The center of the spiral is the snake's head and the pointed end is the tail.

2. Use crayons or markers to decorate the snake.

Cut along line on paper plate

3. Cut along the spiral line.

4. Fasten the thread to the head of the snake and hang it over a radiator or hot air vent. Watch the snake spin as the warm air rises.

warm air

36

The Wind

Wind is created because the Sun warms the Earth unevenly. As warm air expands and rises in some areas, cool air rushes in to take its place. This movement of air is what we call the **wind.** In general, winds blow east or west rather than north or south. That is because Earth's rotation causes the winds to twist to the right or left.

There are three main wind patterns on Earth:

At the equator, the Sun heats the air more than it does over the rest of the globe. This warm air rises high into the atmosphere and moves toward the poles. At the same time, cooler, denser air moves over the Earth's surface toward the equator to replace the heated air. This exchange creates the **trade winds,** which blow in an easterly direction.

At about 30 degrees of latitude, both north and south of the equator, are areas called the **horse latitudes.** Here most of the equatorial air cools and sinks. Some moves back toward the equator, and some moves toward the poles. North of this area the winds blow in a westerly direction.

At about 60 degrees of latitude, both north and south of the equator, the polar air moving toward the equator collides with the warmer air moving in the opposite direction, causing the polar air to rise. This causes the winds to blow in an easterly direction.

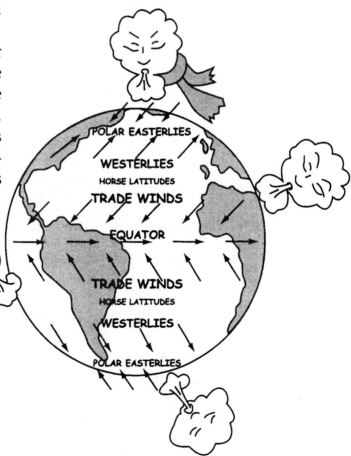

TRADE WINDS

Trade winds blow from the east on both sides of the equator. Using these powerful winds, early explorers were able to sail across the ocean more quickly than at other latitudes. The trade winds of the two hemispheres meet at the equator, where the winds are weak. Sailors call this area the doldrums.

ranged from 0 for complete calm to 12 for a hurricane. Today we have instruments that can measure the actual speed of the wind very precisely, but the Beaufort scale is still useful when no instruments are available.

The windiest place in the United States is the top of Mount Washington in New Hampshire. Wind speeds there have been measured at 231 mph (385 kph)!

Wind Speed

Wind is invisible, but we can "see" it by observing its effect on things around us. In 1806 an Englishman named Sir Francis Beaufort created a system for measuring the strength of the wind. It was based on his observations of the effect wind had on familiar objects. Beaufort's classification

Wind Direction

You may have seen a wind sock at an airport, a flag at the top of a boat mast, or a decorative weather vane on the roof of a house. All these devices help show the direction of the wind. You can make a small weather vane to show which way the wind is blowing.

The Beaufort Scale

Beaufort Scale #	Description	Effect on Land	Wind Speed in mph (kph)
0	calm	smoke goes straight up	less than 1
1	light air	smoke drifts in direction of wind	1–3 (1.5–6)
2	light breeze	wind felt on face; leaves rustle; flags stir; weather vanes turn	4–7 (6.5–11)
3	gentle breeze	leaves and twigs move constantly; light flags blow out	8–12 (13–19)
4	moderate breeze	dust, loose papers, and small branches move; flags flap	13–18 (21–29)
5	fresh breeze	small trees in leaf begin to sway; flags ripple	19–24 (30.5–38.5)
6	strong breeze	large branches in motion; flags beat; umbrellas turn inside out	25–31 (40–50)
7	moderate gale	whole trees in motion; flags are extended	32–38 (51.5–61)
8	fresh gale	twigs break off trees; walking is hard	39–46 (63–74)
9	strong gale	slight damage to houses—TV antennas may blow off, awnings rip	47–54 (75.5–87)
10	whole gale	trees uprooted; much damage to houses	55–63 (88.5–101.5)
11	storm	widespread damage	64–75 (103–121)
12	hurricane	excessive damage	more than 75 (more than 121)

WEATHER VANE

You will need:

scissors
index card
marker or crayon
ruler
drinking straw
white glue
pencil with an eraser
flower pot filled with dirt
straight pin
compass

1. Cut the index card in half. Cut thin triangular shapes off of the two long sides of one half of the card to make a wedge-shape vane as shown. Cut the other half of the index card into four vertical strips. Mark the top of the strips with the letters "N," "S," "E," "W," and set them aside.

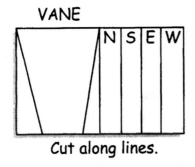

VANE

N S E W

Cut along lines.

2. Make a 1-inch (2.5-cm) slit in one end of a drinking straw. Slip the narrow end of the vane into the slit. Glue in place.

3. Push the pencil into the center of the dirt in the flower pot with the eraser end sticking up.

4. Poke the straight pin through the straw about 2 inches (5 cm) from the vane. Push the end of the pin into the eraser, allowing the straw to rotate freely.

5. Slip the strips marked "N," "S," "E," and "W" into the dirt at the edge of the flower pot to mark the four directions.

6. Place the weather vane in an open area where the wind is not blocked by buildings. Use the compass to align the N, S, E, W markers with the correct directions. Watch the wind push the vane. The other end of the straw will point to the direction from which the wind is blowing.

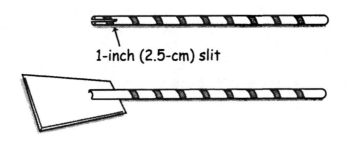

1-inch (2.5-cm) slit

37

Hurricanes and Tornadoes

Hurricanes

Hurricanes are swirling masses of air that may cover an area up to 60 miles (100 km) wide. They form over tropical waters as warm, moist air rises high into the atmosphere. In the northern hemisphere, hurricane winds spin in a counterclockwise direction. In the southern hemisphere, they spin in a clockwise direction. Most of the hurricanes that affect the coasts of the United States occur in the Atlantic. That's because the water along the Pacific coast of the United States is too cold for hurricanes to form. Hurricanes that form in the warm water of the western Pacific Ocean are called typhoons. Those that form over the Bay of Bengal and northern Indian Ocean are called cyclones. Hurricanes, typhoons, and cyclones form most often in summer and fall, when ocean temperatures are the warmest.

Because of their size and duration, hurricanes and the accompanying floods can be the most destructive of all natural disasters. At its peak, a hurricane produces the equivalent energy of half a million atomic bombs. In coastal areas, damage from hurricanes comes from high winds, driving rains, and powerful sea waves that

THE EYE OF THE HURRICANE

Winds near the center of the hurricane move more slowly than those on the perimeter. At the outside edge of the hurricane, wind speeds may reach speeds of 150 miles (241 km) an hour or more. But at the center, or the eye, of the hurricane, the air is calm. The speed of the wind increases with the distance from the center. You can demonstrate why this is so with a Yo-Yo or a button on a string. Hold the end of the string and whirl the Yo-Yo or button around your head. (Do this where there is plenty of room.) Which part of the string is moving faster—the end attached to the Yo-Yo or the end that you are holding?

surge onto the shore. In a terrible hurricane in September 1900, pounding waves literally swept away the coastal city of Galveston, Texas, killing 6,000 people. By the time hurricanes reach inland areas, the wind has usually subsided, but the torrents of rain that the storms still carry often cause disastrous flooding.

Tornadoes

A **tornado** is a violently rotating column of air that descends to the ground during a severe thunderstorm. It has more concentrated destructive power than any other kind of storm. A tornado is like a giant vacuum cleaner that sucks up everything in its path and then blasts it apart. The average tornado is about 660 feet (200 m) wide and travels along the ground at about 30 mph (50 kph). Wind speeds may reach 300 mph (480 kph), although the exact speed is not known because no measuring instrument has yet been made that can withstand the force of a tornado.

Tornadoes are the most uniquely American weather disaster. More tornadoes form in the United States than any other place on Earth. Between 700 and 1,000 tornadoes occur every year. They occur by far the most frequently in the American Midwest, usually in an area known as Tornado Alley. This region covers a broad area including Texas, Oklahoma, Kansas, Nebraska, and Arkansas, plus a part of Louisiana. Texas has an average of 120 tornadoes a year, more than any other state. Other tornado pockets are in Georgia and Alabama, and in Illinois, Indiana, Michigan, and Ohio.

TORNADO WATCH

When weather conditions are likely to produce a tornado, the National Weather Service issues a tornado watch. Anyone in the area should be sure to have a safe place to go in case a tornado warning is issued. A tornado warning means that a tornado has been spotted. If there is a tornado warning for your area, go to a safe place as quickly as possible. The safest place to be in a tornado is on the lowest floor of a building in an inside room or interior hallway. You should cover yourself with pillows or blankets. If you can, get under a sturdy bench.

TORNADO IN A JAR

You will need:

large jar, such as a mayonnaise or peanut
  butter jar
water
spoon
food coloring (blue or green)

1. Fill the jar with water.

2. Use the spoon to stir the water quickly in a circular motion so that the water swirls. Remove the spoon and immediately put a few drops of food coloring into the center of the swirling water.

3. Watch the motion of the colored water. Does it look like a tiny tornado? The revolving air of a tornado is like the swirling water in the jar. The "tornado" in the jar will gradually disappear as the food coloring dissolves in the water.

water

38

Using the Wind

For thousands of years, people have used the power of the wind to turn the sails of windmills. Windmills were used to grind grain, pump water, press oil, saw wood, and to do many other things. During the settlement of the American West, windmills pumped water in remote places that had no other sources of power. Today modern wind machines are being used to harness the energy of the wind and turn it into electricity.

WIND FARMS

In what look like forests of windmills, hundreds of whirling blades are being used to produce electricity on "wind farms" in California and other places. The wind pushes the blades of the wind turbine, or windmill, causing them to turn the shaft of a generator, which produces an electrical current. Up to 30 to 40 percent of the wind's energy can be captured in this way. Wind is a clean, renewable source of energy that will become more important as we use up fossil fuels.

PINWHEEL

You can make a pinwheel and see the power of the wind at work.

You will need:

ruler

pencil

sheet of heavy paper

scissors

crayons or colored markers (optional)

plastic straw

thin nail 1¼ inches (3 cm) long

hammer

thin stick (such as a ¼-inch [0.5-cm] dowel)

1. Use the ruler to measure and draw a 4-inch (10-cm) square on the paper. Cut it out.

2. Following the diagram on page 100, mark the center of the square and a spot about ½" (1 cm) in from each corner. Draw four curved lines as shown. If you want to decorate your pinwheel, use crayons or markers to draw some designs on the paper. Cut along the curved lines.

3. Cut a ½-inch (1.5-cm) length of the plastic straw.

4. With the nail, carefully poke holes in the paper at the marks in the center and at each corner.

5. Lift each corner strip up and bend it toward the center so the four holes

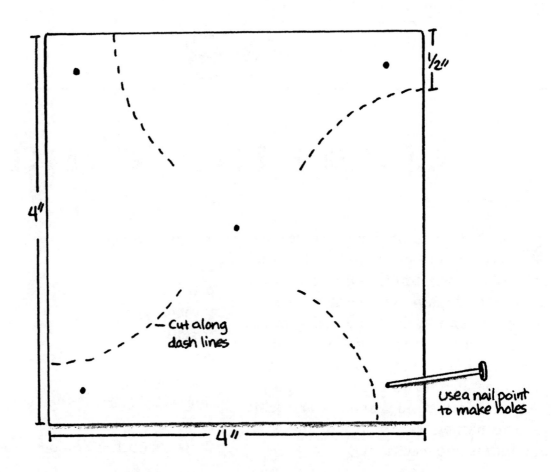

Cut along
dash lines

½"

4"

4"

use a nail point
to make holes

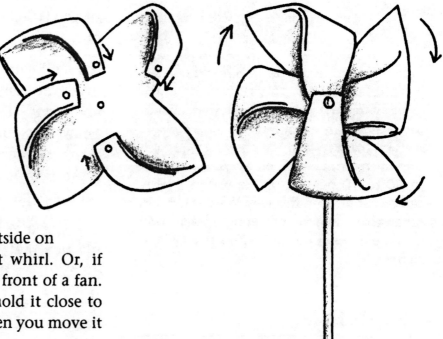

overlap. Put the nail through the four holes and the ½-inch (1.5-cm) straw. Then put the nail through the center hole. Hammer the point of the nail into the stick. Make sure that the pinwheel can turn freely.

6. Take your pinwheel outside on a windy day and watch it whirl. Or, if there is no wind, hold it in front of a fan. What happens when you hold it close to the fan? What happens when you move it farther away?

GLOSSARY

active solar energy system a system that collects heat from the Sun and circulates it through a hot water or heating system.

aerial photo photograph taken from the air looking down at the ground.

Antarctic Circle the line of latitude about 66½ degrees south of the equator.

anthropology the study of humankind. Biological, or physical, anthropology studies the development of the physical and skeletal characteristics and the genetic makeup of humans. Cultural anthropology studies the life-ways of people both ancient and modern.

Arctic Circle the line of latitude about 66½ degrees north of the equator.

atmosphere the layer of gases that surrounds Earth, forming a protective shield from the Sun's harmful radiation.

atmospheric pressure the weight of Earth's atmosphere overhead.

axis an imaginary line running through the center of Earth from the North Pole to the South Pole. The line is tilted 23½ degrees, and this tilting is responsible for Earth's seasons.

barometer a device that measures atmospheric pressure.

basin a depression in Earth's surface. Some basins are filled with water; others are dry most of the time.

bay a small area of a sea or lake partly surrounded by dry land.

biology the study of living things.

butte a tall, steep-sided tower of rock formerly part of a mesa.

canyon a deep, narrow valley with steep sides.

cartographer a mapmaker.

cartography the process of mapmaking.

climate the pattern of weather that one region has over a long period of time.

compass an instrument used to determine directions by means of a free-swinging magnetic needle that always points to magnetic north.

compass rose a flower-like design used to show directions, usually showing 32 points of the compass.

continental divide an elevated boundary that separates rivers flowing toward opposite sides of a continent.

continental drift a theory that the continental landmasses are moving across the Earth.

continents the large landmasses of Earth, including the islands that are associated with them.

contour map also called a topographic map; shows the elevation of the ground.

dam a structure built across a river to control the flow of water.

Daylight Saving Time moves the clock one hour ahead of Sun time.

delta a flat, low-lying plain that sometimes forms at the mouth of a river.

desert an area of land that receives less than 10 inches (25 cm) of precipitation a year.

doldrums area of weak winds close to the equator.

drought a prolonged period of greatly reduced precipitation.

earthquake a shaking of the earth caused by the release of energy as rock suddenly breaks or shifts under stress.

elevation the altitude of land above a reference point, usually sea level.

equator an imaginary line circling Earth at latitude 0 degrees; the starting point for measuring distances north or south on a map or globe.

erosion the movement of weathered materials—rock fragments and particles of soil broken down by water, ice, and temperature changes.

fjord a long, narrow ocean inlet.

fresh water water that is not salty.

geographic pole an imaginary point through which Earth's axis passes.

geography the branch of science that encompasses all aspects of Earth's physical features and inhabitants.

geology the study of the physical history of the Earth, its composition, its structure, and the processes that form and change it.

glacier a huge mass of ice that moves slowly over land.

globe a scale model of Earth.

gores the narrow pointed sections of a globe when they are drawn on a flat surface.

greenhouse effect the warming of Earth's atmosphere through heat absorption.

groundwater water beneath Earth's surface, mainly rain and melted snow that has seeped down through the soil and into pores and cracks in rocks.

hill land that rises above its surroundings and has a rounded summit. A hill is smaller and less rugged than a mountain.

horse latitudes areas about 30 degrees of latitude both north and south of the equator.

hurricane a swirling mass of air that forms over tropical waters as warm, moist air rises high into the atmosphere.

ice sheet a broad, thick layer of glacial ice that covers a large area.

iceberg large chunks of ice that break off, or calve, from glaciers and fall into the sea.

inset a smaller map that appears within a larger map and shows some of the same area, usually in greater detail.

International Date Line a line centered on the 180th meridian that marks the point at which one day ends and a new one begins.

island a body of land that is surrounded by water.

isobars lines connecting regions of the same atmospheric pressure on a weather map.

isotherms lines connecting areas of the same temperature on a weather map.

isthmus a narrow strip of land connecting two larger land areas and separating two bodies of water.

jet stream fast-moving stream of air in the upper atomosphere.

lake a body of water surrounded by land.

latitude an imaginary line circling the globe in an east-west direction. Measured in degrees north and south of the equator.

legend see **map key.**

lodestone see **magnetite.**

longitude imaginary lines circling the globe in a north-south direction. Measured in degrees east or west of the prime meridian.

magnetic pole an imaginary point through which Earth's magnetic axis passes.

magnetite a type of naturally magnetic iron ore; also called a lodestone.

map key an explanation of the symbols used on a map; also called a legend.

meridian another word for line of longitude. The prime meridian is at longitude 0 degrees and runs through Greenwich, England; it is the starting point for measuring distances east or west on a map or globe.

mountain land rising 1,000 feet (300 m) or higher above the surrounding area.

ocean global expanse of water that surrounds the continents.

passive solar energy system a system that relies on natural methods of collecting and distributing heat from the Sun.

peninsula a piece of land jutting out into a lake or into the ocean.

photovoltaic cells devices that convert the Sun's energy into electricity.

plain a large area of relatively flat land, often covered with grasses.

plate tectonics the study of how Earth's plates move and connect.

plateau a large, relatively flat area that stands above the surrounding land.

polar zones regions of the Earth lying between the Arctic Circle and the North Pole and the Antarctic Circle and the South Pole.

precipitation falling moisture from clouds, such as rain, snow, hail, and sleet.

Prime Meridian the starting point for measuring distance both east and west around the globe.

projection the process of transferring information from the curved Earth to a flat surface.

rain liquid precipitation.

relief maps three-dimensional maps of the Earth.

reservoir an artificial lake in which large quantities of water are stored.

rift a crack in Earth's crust where two plates are pulling apart.

river a large natural stream of flowing water.

scale a key on a map that uses a small measure to represent a larger area on the Earth.

sea a large body of water smaller than an ocean that may or may not be part of an ocean.

strait a narrow passage of water that connects two larger bodies of water.

surveying the science of locating the position of points on Earth's surface.

temperate zones the latitudes between the tropics and the polar circles.

thermal upward current of warm air.

tornado a violently rotating column of air that descends to the ground during a severe thunderstorm.

trade winds easterly blowing winds north and south of the equator.

Tropic of Cancer latitude 23½ degrees north.

Tropic of Capricorn latitude 23½ degrees south.

tropical zone region of the Earth lying between the Tropic of Cancer and the Tropic of Capricorn.

tsunami a long, low ocean wave created by an earthquake, landslide, volcanic eruption, or undersea explosion.

valley an elongated natural depression in the Earth bordered by higher land.

volcano a vent, or opening, in Earth's crust that allows molten lava, gases, and other materials to come out of Earth's interior.

water cycle the movement of water between the earth and the air in three stages—evaporation, condensation, and precipitation.

water table the upper portion of water stored in the ground.

water vapor the gaseous form of water.

waterfall a steep descent of a river over a rocky ledge.

weather conditions of the atmosphere at a particular time and place, including temperature, precipitation, air pressure, and wind speed and direction.

wind the motion caused by the movement of air.

FOR FURTHER READING AND MORE PROJECTS

Gardner, Robert. *Science Project Ideas about Rain*. Berkeley Heights, NJ: Enslow Publishers, 1997.

Hewitt, Sally. *Weather*. Brookfield, CT: Copper Beech Books, The Milbrook Press, 1999.

Knowlton, Jack. *Geography from A to Z, a Picture Glossary*. New York, NY: HarperCollins, 1988.

Mandell, Muriel. *Simple Weather Experiments with Everyday Materials*. New York, NY: Sterling Publishing, 1990.

Morris, Scott E., consulting editor. *Using and Understanding Maps: The Endangered World*. Broomall, PA: Chelsea House Publishers, 1993.

Murphy, Bryan. *Experiments with Water*. Minneapolis, MN: Lerner Publications, 1991.

National Geographic Society. *Exploring Your World, the Adventure of Geography*. Washington, DC: National Geographic Society, 1989, 1993, 1995.

Rybolt, Thomas R., and Robert C. Mebane. *Environmental Experiments about Air*. Berkeley Heights, NJ: Enslow Publishers, 1993.

Rybolt, Thomas R., and Robert C. Mebane. *Environmental Experiments about Land*. Berkeley Heights, NJ: Enslow Publishers, 1993.

Van Cleave, Janice. *Geography for Every Kid*. New York, NY: John Wiley & Sons, 1993.

Walpole, Brenda. *Air*. New York/London/Toronto/Sydney: Warwick Press, 1987.

Woelfle, Gretchen. *The Wind at Work: An Activity Guide to Windmills*. Chicago, IL: Chicago Review Press, 1997.

Wyler, Rose. *Science with Mud and Dirt*. New York, NY: Julian Messner, 1986.

Zike, Dinah. *The Earth Science Book*. New York, NY: John Wiley & Sons, 1993.

INDEX